Breaking Point

BY THE SAME AUTHOR

The Boy No One Loved
Crying for Help
Little Prisoners
Too Hurt to Stay
Mummy's Little Helper
Just a Boy (short story)
Breaking the Silence
A Last Kiss for Mummy
Scarlett's Secret (short story)
The Girl Without a Voice
Nowhere to Go
No Place for Nathan
(short story)
A Stolen Childhood
The Wild Child (short story)
Skin Deep

Daddy's Boy (short story)
Mummy's Little Soldier
The Little Princess
(short story)
At Risk (short story)
Runaway Girl
The Silent Witness
Groomed
A Boy Without Hope
A Dark Secret
Let Me Go
Mummy, Please Don't Leave
I Just Want to Be Loved
I Want My Daddy
Little Girl Lost
A Family Friend

CASEY WATSON

Breaking Point

Daniel just wants someone he can rely on.

This book is a work of non-fiction based on the author's experiences. In order to protect privacy, names, identifying characteristics, dialogue and details have been changed or reconstructed.

HarperElement
An imprint of HarperCollins*Publishers*
1 London Bridge Street
London SE1 9GF

www.harpercollins.co.uk

HarperCollins*Publishers*
Macken House, 39/40 Mayor Street Upper
Dublin 1, D01 C9W8, Ireland

First published by HarperElement 2026

1 3 5 7 9 10 8 6 4 2

© Casey Watson 2026

Casey Watson asserts the moral right to
be identified as the author of this work

A catalogue record of this book is
available from the British Library

PB ISBN 978-0-00-877621-3
EB ISBN 978-0-00-877622-0

Printed and bound in the UK using 100%
renewable electricity at CPI Group (UK) Ltd

All rights reserved. No part of this publication may be reproduced, stored in a retrieval system, or transmitted, in any form or by any means, electronic, mechanical, photocopying, recording or otherwise, without the prior written permission of the publishers.

Without limiting the exclusive rights of any author, contributor or the publisher of this publication, any unauthorised use of this publication to train generative artificial intelligence (AI) technologies is expressly prohibited. HarperCollins also exercise their rights under Article 4(3) of the Digital Single Market Directive 2019/790 and expressly reserve this publication from the text and data mining exception.

Dedication

I dedicate this book to all my readers who have ever been in care. It is not something we would wish for, but so often it's the only way. I know many of you had your lives transformed by a caring foster family, but some have had less positive experiences. I hope that you can find strength when looking back and continue to live happy and fulfilling lives, and that if you're ever in a dark place you'll reach out and talk to someone, because there is always somebody who wants to listen.

Sending love, Casey x

Acknowledgements

As ever, I have some important people to thank: my fabulous agent, Andrew Lownie, and the incredible team at HarperCollins, my publishing family, whose skill and expertise continue to bring these stories to you so brilliantly.

I must also give thanks to my friend and partner-in-writing-crime, Lynne Barrett-Lee. We've become such a team now that we can almost finish one another's sentences. And often do … when we're not busy writing, that is.

Once again, I cannot pass up the opportunity to thank my amazing family and friends, who continue to keep me sane, and support me in myriad ways. I simply could not do what I do without you.

Finally, I'd once again like to acknowledge all of you, my lovely readers. Your kind reviews really are all the encouragement I need to keep sharing stories of these so often forgotten children. You are the best. I send my love to you all.

Chapter 1

April

It goes without saying that life happens when you're busy making other plans, because a lot of the time, that is, of course, true. And when the phone rings – well, you're usually doing something else, aren't you? Leaving aside lovelorn teenagers, famous for mooning around in their bedrooms, positively willing the phone *to* ring, most of us, when it does, tend to be occupied. Watching the TV, doing the ironing, hurrying to make the school run … Or, in this case, carefully manoeuvring a car out of a parking space, which was too small when we entered it (it was the only one we could find in the multi-storey), and was so small when we returned to it (another, bigger car having now parked adjacent to it) that, until we moved it, only one of us could even get in.

In this case it was me, being the small one in our marriage, clambering across the passenger seat to get behind the wheel and leaving Mike with the job of making sure that, while I reversed back out of the parking space, no car would get scratched in the process.

'Honestly!' he huffed, as I inched minutely backwards. 'I mean, what about people who've got casts on, or something? Or are disabled, or—'

'Love, keep an eye on the bumper!'

'Sorry – left hand down a bit. Just a fraction. Go *slowly*!'

'I *am* going slowly!'

'Not slowly enough! There you go. Now straight. Keep coming … keep coming … Just be mindful of the pillar once you're level with the wing mirrors …'

'Bloody pillars,' I huffed back. 'Who designs these flipping car parks? I mean, can it really be beyond the brains of car park designers not to put the pillars between the parking spaces?'

'Clearly not. Keep coming …'

'What about the other side? How close am I?'

'Bags of room that side. Just keep your eye on the wing mirror …'

'I *am looking* in the wing mirror!'

'Yes, but the *edge* of it. You have fag papers, literally …'

That was the moment when Christine Bolton called, which meant I had to let it go to voicemail. It was also around half an hour since we'd finished our appointment with Mike's lovely lady surgeon and were bringing home news that was both welcome and unwelcome – that my poor husband was going to have to have his knee replaced.

It was welcome, of course, because the knee had been troubling him for some time now and to be out of pain would be a wonderful thing. But also unwelcome because, well, how could it not be? There'd be the operation itself – Mike, famously, 'didn't do' hospitals – plus the aftermath, the rehabilitation, the potential weeks away from work. And all of that just to get back to the place where he'd started: with a knee functioning well enough that he could go back to playing football. 'Proper football', as he'd put it, rather than doing as he had been since he'd twisted it so badly – his nemesis: the dreaded 'going in goals'. And I felt for him. It was a situation that had genuinely shocked him. 'But I'm only 58!' he had told the surgeon plaintively. But a lifetime playing sport – and getting injured – had apparently taken its toll. Plus, look on the bright side, the surgeon had pointed out. Being so young, and so fit (Mike had sat up straighter in his chair then), meant he'd find the whole process a breeze.

'I don't know about "breeze",' he said now, having clambered back into the passenger seat of the finally released vehicle. 'I feel like I've just been hit by a tsunami.'

'I know, love,' I said. 'But it is what it is. And at least it sounds as though you won't have too long to wait.'

'That's what worries me!' he replied. Then he shuddered involuntarily. 'The thought of going under the knife …'

'I know, love,' I said. 'But you know it's for the best. And in the meantime, we'll just have to find ways to take your mind off it.'

Which was when my mobile trilled a second time: Christine again. And this time I took the call that, quite apart from anything else, was definitely going to do just that.

'Oh! You're there!' Christine said. 'I'm so sorry to keep badgering you only I hadn't left a voice message and thought perhaps I should. I'm off into a meeting soon and I didn't want to leave it as I'm out of the office tomorrow. And anyway, you've answered so now I won't need to. So that's good. Are you okay to talk?'

She sounded a little flustered, which was not my supervising social worker's usual style.

'Everything okay?' I asked.

'Yes, yes, I'm fine. Are you driving?'

'I am,' I said. 'Don't worry though, you're on speaker and we're just about to join the rush hour snail-crawl in any case. You have a child for us?'

'I do. A teenager, lad of 15. He's currently in a children's home.' She named one I was familiar with. 'But things are spiralling a little rapidly out of control.'

I could sense Mike's involuntary grimace out of the corner of my eye. 'In what way?' I asked Christine.

Breaking Point

'The usual. Mostly drugs. He's been hanging out more and more with some of the older kids who live there and he's now also getting involved with a local county lines gang. Drug dealing, petty crime ... all the things you'd expect. So, the manager there is keen to see if we can have another go at finding a family setting for him, break the cycle before it's too late.'

'Why now? Has he been in foster care before? What's his story?'

'He's been in the children's home for around three years now, pretty much his whole time in care. He was fostered initially – twice, in fact. But the placements didn't work out. He was apparently already too much of a handful.'

'And before that?'

'Absent mother. Dad in prison for drugs offences. No family, bar an uncle, who took him in briefly but chucked him out. You know, same old, same old,' Christine added, with a sigh. 'Poor lad's been dealt a pretty rotten hand. Anyway, the thing is, we know we're going to need a particularly robust family to take him on, so—'

'You thought of us,' I finished for her while, at the same time, Mike couldn't help but add a wry chuckle.

'Is that you, Mike?' Christine asked.

'It is indeed,' he answered. 'I was just laughing at the timing of your use of the word "robust".'

'We've just left the hospital,' I explained. 'Mike's on the waiting list for a knee replacement.' I'd already told

Christine about his knee problems when we'd chatted a couple of weeks previously, so she was aware that it might come to that.

'Oh,' she said now. 'So that's good news, isn't it? Well, when you get to have it, anyway, Mike. But in the meantime, maybe …'

'In the meantime, it's business as usual,' Mike said firmly, glancing in my direction. 'I'm not an invalid – just have to chow down a few more painkillers than usual.'

I could tell he was bridling at the idea that he might be considered less than robust. And he was right to. He'd never been one for giving in to weaknesses, which was probably why he went back to playing too soon after his injury. But that was a discussion for another day, clearly. 'When you say "robust",' I asked Christine, 'in what way do you mean? Is he particularly hard to deal with?'

'To be honest? I'd say yes. He's got a lot of street smarts, a lot of attitude. He needs boundaries to be rigorously enforced. Needs experienced carers. I know everyone does their best at the home, but you know what it's like. There's the lack of continuity. Young, inexperienced staff. Lots of comings and goings. A tendency to naivety … It's all too easy for these kinds of kids to run rings round some of the staff there. So yes,' she added, 'it's exactly why we thought of you two.' Then, after a pause, 'Tell you what? Shall I send over his file? Gives you a chance to take a closer look once you're home and we can catch up again the day after tomorrow, say?'

'Yes, of course,' I said, absolutely no alarm bells ringing, even quietly. After all, we agreed, once the phone had disconnected, we'd looked after seemingly out-of-control teenage boys many times before.

'Though why do I get the feeling,' Mike asked, as we continued our walking-pace way out of town, 'that there was a particularly strong air of profound relief in Christine's voice? I mean, I know she was going to a meeting, but she didn't even pause for breath long enough to tell us what his name is!'

Daniel James O'Connor, it turned out. That was his name.

The sense that the long, languid days of the school summer holidays were behind us – evidenced by that interminable rush-hour journey home – was soon dispelled once we were back in the house and had thrown open the doors to the back garden. It was bathed in dappled sunlight, the heavy flowerheads of Mike's beloved dahlias (his latest passion) nodding their approval as a still-balmy breeze wound its way lazily through their stems. I made coffee and, while Mike wrestled the lawn mower from the shed, pulled out my laptop to see what Christine had sent us.

It was unusual, though not unknown, to have access to so much information about a potential new placement so early on, but unlike the situation where one had just come into care, when a child had been in the system a long time, like this lad, it was easy – this being the twenty-first century – for comprehensive digital records to be available at the click of a button, sent via a secure link, straight to my inbox.

I took my laptop out onto the patio and placed it on the outside table.

'You want to take a look at all this with me?' I asked Mike as I pulled out a chair.

'No time like the present, I suppose,' he said, coming over to join me. 'I imagine we know what to expect.'

Twenty minutes or so later, however, as the breeze became chillier, we both had pause for thought. *Did we?*

Daniel's early story was, sadly, the kind of thing we had seen many times before. As Christine had told us, he'd been living in a children's home since the age of 12, but what a torrid first 12 years of childhood he had lived. Though there was almost nothing about the circumstances that preceded it, his first loss – perhaps the biggest – was that of his mum, who had apparently left the family home when he was eight. She had disappeared in the middle of the night and had never been back. Not that his father had made any attempt to look for her. Indeed, it seemed he had actively refused to even try, it being recorded that he had told his son that if she ever showed up, he would kill her. There was nothing in the file, either, that indicated what the catalyst for that was, though given the poor child had disclosed that both his parents, as well as using drugs, also sold them around their estate, and that 'Dad hit Mum all the time', common sense suggested she had reason enough to leave. But, even with the drug use, the maternal bond is often strong, so why hadn't she escaped *with* her son? It was a mystery that, sadly, we would probably never solve.

In the meantime, O'Connor senior continued to bring his son up himself and, perhaps unsurprisingly, it wasn't that long before things started unravelling. Daniel was recorded as having missed a lot of school and it was normal for him to be up late at night, answering the door to all and sundry, to collect drugs or drop off money. By the time he was 10, he was apparently scooting round the local area himself, joining the family 'business' and dropping off drugs to grateful customers. Then, when he was in Year 6, his final year in primary, the school decided to intervene.

It was nearing the summer holidays at this time, and, with the move to the local secondary happening that September, the school felt they needed to stage a major intervention, to try and get him back on track before the move. The feeling was that if they could be really robust with school attendance and just *get him through* into high school, he might finally get his head down – in a place where everyone else would be older and bigger and his 'top boy' status in the primary was no more.

At this point, with Daniel having been absent for three days with no phone calls or explanation, they sent the local authority education welfare officer round to do

Casey Watson

a welfare check. Daniel himself answered the door to them and, to their astonishment, continued brazenly smoking a cannabis joint while explaining that his dad was asleep and 'mustn't be woken up, or I'll get it'. The education welfare officer, who had noted that the boy seemed not to understand that a ten-year-old smoking cannabis was, to put it mildly, highly unusual, naturally phoned his manager immediately, who informed the local police.

They arrived within minutes and Mr O'Connor was duly woken up. Then, to Daniel's apparent surprise, his father was arrested. They were both taken to the police station and while Dad was obviously headed for the cells, social services were called in to take care of Daniel and he was placed with respite carers temporarily.

As a search of the family home revealed both a great deal of cash and a large quantity of Class A drugs, it was clear Daniel's father would not be going home to look after his son any time soon – indeed, he was probably looking at a lengthy prison sentence, so a new home needed to be found for the boy. And when an uncle suggested himself – Mr O'Connor's younger brother – it was agreed, the usual checks having been made into the man's suitability, that the boy could go and live with him.

It turned out the uncle was almost as bad as his brother, however; also involved in drugs and alcohol, and none too keen on his nephew. He'd only agreed to have him because he relied on his brother's drugs and money, and was only expecting to have to look after Daniel for a few weeks. Four months later, though, when it seemed certain that Mr O'Connor would be locked up for at least six years, he kicked Daniel, now aged just 11, out onto the streets, fearing that he'd have social services sniffing around into his own criminal activities, which had thus far gone under the radar.

Daniel, though streetwise, didn't know what to do with this unexpected curveball. The local junkies – his former clients – now wanted nothing to do with him and everyone he turned to refused to help him. After two days of sleeping in a local park, Daniel, exhausted and very hungry, did something he hated doing: he went to the local police station in the hope of getting help. But brought up to hate and avoid the police at all costs, he presented as angry and rude.

Social services were duly called and he was once again placed in foster care, and Christine's use of the word 'handful' seemed more than justified. He was forced to leave the first family after threatening to throw their seven-year-old daughter down the stairs, and during the second placement, he had taken a hammer to the couple's large wall-mounted TV and, in a rage, smashed it to pieces in front of them. At that point, with no family willing to take him on – this had been during the pandemic, which hadn't helped – he'd been moved into the children's home, a place usually reserved for, and filled to capacity with, teenagers. Daniel, at his point, had not even been 12.

The rest read exactly as both Mike and I expected. Far from becoming another sad statistic in the sorry world of drugs, crime and childhood neglect, Daniel had, at least to his mind, been thriving there. Forget all the adults who were pulling their hair out, Daniel was evidently happy there. He didn't want to leave, having found his natural tribe.

There were other notes, many of them, none of which inspired confidence. A big lad, he looked and acted older than his years. He was prone to throwing his weight around with those smaller and weaker, and there were several violent outbursts recorded. His gravitation towards older males was also cited as a worry; the home's principal reason for pushing for a foster family was to get him right away from those kinds of influences.

As Christine noted, this really was a sad example of 'same old, same old' – a little boy who'd suffered the loss of his mum, gross neglect from his father, rejection from the only family member he really knew and who had subsequently headed down the usual spiral we'd seen so many times before. The forsaken child was now an out-of-control, angry adolescent, one at odds with authority and completely lacking boundaries. But did Mike and I have it in us to turn his life around?

'Gut instinct?' I asked Mike as I flipped the lid closed on my laptop.

He paused for a moment, sighed and then ran a hand across his jaw. 'That he's likely to be trouble?' was his eventual response. 'But it's your shout,' he told me. 'It sounds like the kid could really use a break, doesn't it? And if you're up for it, I am as well.' He smiled. 'As you already know.'

And for a moment I was. This was familiar territory for us, after all. And, well, you had to see behind the behaviours, didn't you? Think of the wretched little lad inside that volatile teen. See hope, and a future, and give him a chance. But then Mike stretched out his bad leg and I caught a wince. Almost nothing, it was. Minuscule. Just a slight furrowing of his brows.

And just like that, I was certain no more. I'd been able to hold my own against all sorts of big, aggressive lads down the years; once you put boundaries in place, set the house rules, made sure that consequences were always, *always* followed through on, your authority could generally, in time, be established. But I'd always had that comfort blanket to fall back on – Mike's place in the equation. The fact that he could always step in if things turned violent or threatening. Just his sheer physical presence in the house. I could count on the fingers of one hand how many times he'd actually had to do that over the years, but what we'd just read seemed almost a guarantee that clipping this boy's wings would be a recipe for disaster – and almost certainly of the physical kind. Could I really allow Mike's health to be put at risk in that way? No way would I do that.

'I'm not sure he's for us,' I said. 'Much as I feel for the lad, I think we should pass. I mean, suppose you get a date for your op through?'

'Then he'd go into respite. Love, I'm not an invalid,' Mike added, as if reading my thoughts. 'And we both know what the waiting lists for ops are right now – I'll be lucky if I get a date by the middle of next year.'

'I know that,' I said. 'But my gut's still saying no. We've stepped up a zillion times before, Christine knows that. Bottom line, she probably already *knows* this isn't right for us.'

'True enough,' Mike conceded. 'And as I say, it's your call. Your decision, love.' He stood up. 'And now I'm going to go and cut the grass.'

And I would need to head inside and let Christine know. But, bad as I felt for her – and the boy – would anyone else take him on? In truth, I doubted it – I knew that I'd made the right decision. Let my sensible head rule my heart for a change.

Well, or so I thought.

Chapter 2

Having got hold of Christine and told her that we weren't able to take Daniel, I very swiftly put the whole thing out of my mind. She'd been understanding, of course. In fact, she'd already had her own reservations, she admitted. 'I wouldn't want it on my conscience, to be honest,' she'd told me. 'Had you not called when you had, I would have called you to say so. It's too much for you both when Mike's in limbo with his injury. There'll be another child.' She laughed. 'There is always another child, eh?'

There was indeed. And in the meantime, I had plenty to do as it was a busy time of year for Watson birthdays. Having just celebrated our son Tyler's 23rd, and our granddaughter Dee Dee's 8th, we had two more coming along in quick succession. October would see mine, plus my youngest grandson, Carter's. Not sure how the time had passed so quickly, but he'd be four. And at least one of us was expecting the whole birthday works – games, balloons, a face-painter, a big bouncy castle and a cake cleverly fashioned into The Incredible Hulk. 'And what's happening at Carter's?' Mike had quipped.

I would, of course, be deliriously happy just to have my entire family around me – even if it was just for some takeaway pizzas. With everyone busy with their own lives, and Tyler and his partner Naomi living some way away, this would be no small achievement in itself. And with my son Kieron and his wife Lauren both working full time now, I was definitely more than happy not to worry about my own age and instead help organise Carter's party. (To which, as is the way now – how did that happen? – his entire class had of course been invited. No 'six kids round for tea' setup these days.)

We were still available for fostering though, be it long term or respite, and the following Thursday morning, I took another call from Christine. She was hoping to find a home for a teenage girl that coming weekend, a 14-year-old, whose name was Bella.

'Just from teatime Friday till Monday morning,' she explained. 'She was supposed to be moving into her new foster home tomorrow, but a family illness means they can't take her now till Monday and her room at the children's home has already been re-allocated – to a lad currently languishing in police custody, unfortunately. Plus, she's all set to go. Could you and Mike take her for the weekend?'

As I had little on at the weekend bar shopping for party bag contents, I assured Christine that we'd be able to take the girl in, so 24 hours later, after a quick refresh of our spare bedroom, Bella arrived, accompanied by her young, smiley social worker, Ellie Pearson. A pretty little thing, Bella had also brought two suitcases, one rucksack and a holdall, those being the sum total of her possessions.

Ellie hugged Bella warmly. They seemed very close. 'So, I'll be back round at eight thirty, Monday morning,' she told us both. 'Well, traffic permitting, that is. Now I really have to fly. You have fun!' Upon which she was back in her car and off up the road, leaving the shy teenager and I to bring all her stuff inside.

'It's really kind of you to have me, Mrs Watson,' Bella said politely. 'I was so upset when I found out I couldn't go to my new family till after the weekend. The thought of having to stay in that place a moment longer …'

'I hear you, love,' I told her. 'And it's Casey, no formalities here. And my husband's called Mike. You'll meet him in an hour or so, once he gets home from work. In the meantime, let's get your stuff up to your bedroom and get you settled in, shall we? Do you like chicken curry?' I asked, as she followed me up the stairs, having insisted on lugging the largest of the two cases. 'Homemade,' I added. 'I'm trying to clear out my freezer. Got a couple of parties coming up so I need to get baking.'

'Oh, I *love* curry,' she said and she sounded like she meant it. 'I like most things, actually. And cooking. I'm really excited to go to my new family – they said I can help out – and cooking for my grandparents too. I think I might like to be a chef.'

So far, so good. And I was pleased that this chatty smiley teen was soon off to be with what sounded like a loving family. Christine had given me enough of a snapshot of Bella's situation that I'd know what I was dealing with, and though from my own point of view it was good to know she was unlikely to present any challenges, her story couldn't help but make me feel sad. She'd come into care five years back, after the untimely death of her single mother from breast cancer, and with Mum having been an only child and her own parents quite elderly, there'd been no family able to take her in. There was apparently a great-aunt several hundred miles away, which had been mooted as a possibility, but since a move to live with her would take her too far away from her loving grandparents it had been decided, in conjunction with Bella herself, of course, that foster care locally would represent a better solution since she'd still be able to see her nan and grandad regularly.

Happily, a lovely family had stepped up. A slightly older couple who, like so many once their own kids had flown the nest – in this case, a daughter – had wanted to do something worthwhile with their time. And indeed, they did. But, after Bella had spent a very happy four years with them, tragedy had once again come calling. Her foster dad had died suddenly, of a heart attack, leaving his wife totally bereft, and with their own daughter having by now relocated to the other end of the country with her job, Mum had decided to sell up and move there as well. She was keen that Bella go too, of course, but that would once again mean her being separated from her grandparents, who had, by now, moved into a supported living complex nearby. Understandably, she couldn't bear to leave them.

Difficult as it was for all concerned, a new foster home obviously had to be found for Bella, but they had been struggling to find a suitable family local to the grandparents, hence her having to move into a children's home. It was always only going to be a temporary measure, but by now she had been living there for four months – and could not wait, it transpired, to get out of there.

'It's just horrible,' she told me, once we were back downstairs and I'd made her a mug of tea. 'The only place I feel safe – when I'm not at school – is when I'm in my room, with the door locked. There's comings and goings at all times of the night and stuff gets pinched all the time, and no one seems to even care. Well, they do, but the people that work there aren't even that much older than some of the lads! If they'd not managed to find anywhere for me to move on to, I was getting to the point where I think I would have run away anyway.'

I could only sympathise and commiserate with the poor girl. And it made me beyond glad that we'd been able to take her in. Among the handful of homes that were dotted around our area, this was a story that was depressingly familiar.

* * *

It wasn't until the Sunday evening that I put two and two together. Since our conversations had understandably centred more on Bella's frail-sounding grandparents, and the horrible decision she'd had to make not to head south with her loving foster mum, we'd not really spoken further about the lonely and stressful few months she'd endured at the children's home. Everything was about the future – the hopes she had of settling in with her new foster mum and the GCSEs she was about to start studying for. It was the arrival of a text that would go on to make me think, one that came in just after we'd finished tea.

It had caused her to chuckle.

'Look,' she said, showing me the screen on her mobile. It was a photo of a young lad, dark-haired, and gurning manically at the camera. He'd used one of those silly filters kids these days are forever playing about with, causing his eyes to appear massive and filling his mouth with similarly enormous cartoon teeth. There was a message flashing too, which said 'already miss you, belly-boo!'

'He's such an idiot,' she said affectionately. 'I'm not going to miss anything about that horrible place,' she added, 'but I'm definitely going to miss him.'

'Who's that?' I asked.

'Deejay. My friend.' She began texting him back, in that mind-bogglingly fast way youngsters were able to. Engaging in conversation with me while her hands managed to fly simultaneously across the little keyboard, operating seemingly all by themselves. 'He always had my back,' she said. 'It would have been a million times worse in there if he hadn't looked after me. You know, protecting me from the older lads. Keeping them away from me. Stopping me from being bullied. Making sure my stuff didn't get nicked.'

As was so often the case, the picture she painted sounded almost Dickensian, the children's home less a home than a lawless Wild West. I knew experiences differed, as did homes, of course. I also knew the majority of those who worked in them tried to do their very best. But the three local ones I'd had experience of over the years I'd been fostering hadn't exactly conjured a particularly rosy picture. How could they? The best place for any child is within a loving, supportive family – something a children's home, for all their best intentions (and I definitely did believe those in the sector had absolutely the best intentions), was always going to find challenging to replicate. It was no wonder children often felt isolated, anxious and lonely, and if they did form relationships, with either staff members or fellow housemates, the transient nature of life in such places made every bond feel so much more fragile. So, much as I was happy she'd soon be back with a family, the fact that Bella had at least made a friend there was heartwarming.

'Well, you two can definitely keep in touch,' I said, pointing towards her mobile. 'That's one of the great things about our modern hyper-connected world, isn't it?' To which she nodded, though it occurred to me that this was the only one she knew – one where you could speak to anyone, anywhere in the world, at any time. Not always a good thing, in my opinion, and I knew lots felt similarly, but, in this case, a definite plus. She'd also be able to keep in touch with the foster family she'd left, of course – to which point our conversation naturally moved on.

Which is probably why it was a while before it occurred to me, given that there were several children's homes locally, that she might well have been at the same one as the lad we'd just turned down. Had he been one of those scary older lads her friend Deejay had shielded her from? Who'd made her feel unsafe, who'd been mean and threatening to her, who'd perhaps tried to nick her stuff? Given what I knew of him, it wouldn't have surprised me. I knew from what I'd read about him that he probably ticked every box. It served to remind me that we'd probably made the right decision.

Confidentiality meant there was no way it would be permissible to ask Bella, but later that evening, when she and Deejay had exchanged more jokey texts, I did venture to ask her about the lad she'd grown so fond of. Was he, like her, stuck in a sad, unhappy place, trying to make the best of a grim situation?

'Has he been there a very long time, this Deejay?' I asked her.

'Ages,' she said. She shook her head and sighed. 'I feel so bad for him. He's got no family at *all*. It's so sad.'

'It's very sad,' I agreed. 'Must be tough for him.'

'It's really hard,' she said. 'He said they've been trying to find a family for him, but they've not had any luck yet. He said no one wants to take teenage boys, especially ones from children's homes. I feel so sorry for him.'

I felt a small twinge of guilt, knowing Mike and I were among that number. That said, we'd certainly taken on our share of challenging teenage boys in the past and it had often proved entirely as billed. It was also a story I had heard many, many times before. Teenage boys, particularly very troubled ones, were always hard to place – and as time went by, it only ever got harder for them. Which was why, at the time, I could do little more than sympathise. But at least he'd found a confidante in Bella – a friendship that might continue. As could ours, I assured her before she left the following morning, off to settle into what would hopefully represent a positive step for her and allow her to continue seeing her grandparents regularly.

It was only the following day that another possible scenario sprang to mind. I took another call from Christine on the Monday morning, shortly after Bella left, and though we'd been talking about other things, mostly a couple of upcoming training courses we'd been encouraged to sign up for, I did think to ask her if the home Bella been staying in was the same one as Daniel O'Connor. Given there were only a handful of children's homes locally, there was obviously a reasonably high chance that it was. 'What she told me of it made me think,' I said, outlining the issues with aggressive older boys there, which almost certainly could have included him. 'It all sounded very similar to what I read in Daniel's notes.'

A few clicks later and Christine was able to confirm it. 'You're right,' she said. 'Same home. Poor girl, no wonder she was so relieved to be placed back with a family. Must have been a pretty grim few months for her.'

I agreed. It didn't sound like a nice environment for an anxious 14-year-old girl. 'She did at least make a friend, though, which she said helped a lot. A lad called Deejay, who she seemed to have struck up a real rapport with. So that's a plus. Just a shame, from what she told me, that he's unlikely to be as lucky as she has. Unless … What's his story? Are you involved?'

'I don't think so,' she said. 'The name's definitely not familiar. I suppose it's possible we're not actively looking to move him.' I could hear clicking as she presumably pulled up some information 'Hang on,' she said. 'What did you say the lad's name was?'

'Deejay, she said,' I answered.

'Deejay? Good lord!'

'What?'

'But – yes, yes, I'm sure – that *is* Daniel O'Connor. As in Daniel *James* O'Connor. As in DJ, to his friends. That's his nickname.'

'*Really*?' I was aghast. 'But I never saw that in his notes.'

Breaking Point

'Well, it's right on the screen in front of me. I'm looking at his family search profile and it's there: "Known as DJ to his friends". Got to be the same person, got to be.'

'I'm staggered,' I said. 'Genuinely. The lad she described to me sounded like a completely different boy.'

'Well,' she said, 'I suppose everyone has more than one side to them, don't they? If we're talking about the same kid, that is – though I can't imagine we're not. There are only nine kids in that home in total. Anyway, I have to dash now. Just let me know which course dates you can do once you've had a chat with Mike, yes?'

I promised I would, but now I couldn't put it out of my mind. Had I really been barking up the wrong tree all weekend? Jumping to what had seemed such a reasonable conclusion, that the lad we'd turned down had been one of Bella's tormentors, when, in fact, the opposite was true?

'It's really knocked me for six,' I told Mike once he'd got home from work. 'If it's true – and I have to accept it is, because it must be him, mustn't it? – the lad really looked out for the poor girl. I feel bad now for judging him so negatively.'

'Love, *hardly*. You – we – just acted on the information we'd been given. And Christine felt the same, don't forget. He's not the right lad for us – not right now, anyway. We went with our instincts and our instincts don't generally let us down.' Then he paused.

'What? Come on, spit it out. You've changed your mind, haven't you?'

I have no time for bullies. Doesn't matter that I know – as do many in my line of work – that bullying results from some kind of lack in the bully, not the bullied. No matter that we all know they are to be pitied more than feared. I never have had time for bullying, no exceptions. However, those who *stand up* to bullies, those people I have all the time in the world for. Because standing up to bullies is a brave but hard thing to do. And even more so when you step up to do it for others, because that involves empathy – the antithesis of that awful mantra, 'every man for himself'. A kid who could do that could not be all bad.

I winced very slightly under my husband's close scrutiny.

'Yes, love,' I told him. 'You know, I think I have. He deserves a chance, doesn't he? At least a fair hearing.'

The following Monday afternoon, we took in Daniel James O'Connor.

Chapter 3

One thing was clear. While we had had a change of heart about giving Daniel O'Connor a chance, we were not taking this placement on lightly. Prior to his arrival, therefore, I had a long phone conversation with Christine about some lingering reservations I still had.

'I mean, I'm not in the slightest bit naive, Christine, as you know,' I said, 'and yes, after hearing Bella's perspective on the lad, I still feel bad about writing him off so readily before. But I still have some concerns.'

'Oh God, yes, of course you must have,' Christine agreed. 'I'd be more worried if you didn't, to be honest. Rest assured though, Casey, it goes without saying that any extra support you might need, you've only got to ask and it'll be there. Truth is, there's simply nobody else who will take him on. And that's absolutely not to pressure you, it's just a sad bloody fact.'

'I get it, I really do,' I said, 'and of course I'll ask if I need help, I'd be an idiot not to. I'm just more concerned that we are now uprooting him from his "manor", aren't we? His comfort zone – where he's some kind of modern-day Fagin, by all accounts.'

Christine laughed at that. 'I know what you mean, Casey,' she said, 'but I think he's more Oliver Twist than Fagin. He's the one doing all the running for others, according to police reports, but you're right, initially he's not going to like being lifted out of his little kingdom. Which is all the more reason to do so. I'm hoping though that, like most teens that pass through your doors, he'll see there's more to life and maybe settle down at last.'

I paused before continuing as I knew Christine and her manager were really desperate to place this lad.

'Okay, so what we've decided is that although we are saying yes, we want it on record that this is going to be a trial period. A month, we thought, and if in the meantime we can see that it's definitely not going to work, for whatever reason – be it Mike's health, or the lad's behaviour – we can walk away without this being recorded as a failed placement.'

This was important. A failed placement now and again wasn't too much of a big deal, but senior managers looked closely at carers who had too many on their records and during an annual review, they'd be asked to explain them. It obviously wasn't a given, but it often seemed, at least to me, that blame and fault when this happened seemed to always lie with the carer, so I was naturally keen to avoid this wherever possible.

'Of course we can do that, it's more than generous,' Christine said, the relief in her voice now apparent. 'And then, after that first month, if it's all going well, we can say that it is to be reviewed on a month-by-month basis. Would that work for you both?'

'That's perfect,' I said, 'but Daniel will need to be told this, too. I know it will only add to his troubles – not knowing that he's got a permanent home yet – but given the circumstances, I think it's necessary. Feel free to blame it on Mike's health, if it comes to it. Might be easier. But that's the best we can offer right now.'

'Absolutely,' Christine agreed, 'and no, we won't blame it on Mike. We will make it clear to Daniel that he's on trial with you guys. It might actually help concentrate his mind. You never know. And it's not like he's a young lad who won't be able to take that kind of ultimatum – far from it.'

'Though if he wants out – back to his little fiefdom – he knows playing us up might achieve that so I do know it might prove to be counterproductive.'

'True enough,' Christine agreed. 'But let's be positive. We're giving him a chance, and if, ultimately, he chooses not to take it, at least we know we've done what we could.'

So, it was settled and Daniel would be joining us the following afternoon. And I resolved to be exactly that – positive. Bella obviously believed that, deep down, he'd prefer to be with a family, so all the cock-of-the-walk swagger I'd read about, well, perhaps that was just a front to give him status among his peers. The little lad was still in there, after all.

In the meantime, a new placement could only mean one thing: making the house gleam and doing a bedroom transformation. So, while Mike was out, watching some football tournament or other with our son Kieron, I got busy cleaning and re-arranging. The bits I'd put out for Bella in the spare room had to go, of course. No teenage boy would put up with fluffy pink and cream cushions and a matching duvet, with complementary teddy bears and assorted smellies. It all got bundled up and either added to the laundry piles or put away in the huge cupboards along the landing, after which I started my search for more suitable things.

All I had to go on was that Daniel liked gaming – he was PlayStation mad apparently – oh, and rap music. My favourite kind. Not. I grimaced at the Alexa speaker I'd recently bought for children to use in that bedroom and made a mental note to discuss volumes as soon as I showed the lad around.

The search for bedding proved difficult. My grandson Levi, who would be 17 soon, had gone through a PlayStation phase, but once I dug out the gamer duvet cover we'd bought for him, I decided against putting it out – it just looked too childish for this hardened, street-wise lad. After another 20 minutes of rummaging through the airing cupboard I finally settled on a plain dark grey set, topped off with a couple of black cushions. Not my usual style, but it was the best I could come up with and I had an inkling he'd barely notice anyway.

I was still at it when Mike arrived home and bounded up the stairs. 'I can't smell anything,' he said, sniffing the air theatrically. 'What's for dinner?'

As usual when on a cleaning mission, I had entirely lost track of the time. Time to think on my feet.

'Your favourite takeaway,' I said. 'I thought I'd put the order in to the Chinese while you're in the bath, then we can settle down with it and enjoy our final night of peace.'

'Come on, Case! You forgot. Been too busy up here doing your Mary Poppins' thing, haven't you?'

I smiled. 'Busted!' I said. 'But I fancy Chinese anyway. And we can continue with the freezer clearance tomorrow. Oh, but before that, could you spare me 10 minutes?'

Which, of course, turned into 30 as I had my poor tired husband lugging a black office chair from the garden shed (sorry, workshop!) up to the spare room and then helping me carry a black desk from the snug, which we never really used, up there to join the chair.

'There!' I said, standing back to admire the newly refurbished room. 'A proper gamer's room this is now, don't you think? Maybe some of those stick-on coloured light things all the teenagers are into and that will complete the look.'

Mike shook his head wearily. 'Whatever you think, love. I'm off to run my bath before you decide to have me bring up the bloody kitchen sink!'

I was still feeling pleased with myself the following lunchtime as I paced between the living room and kitchen areas and waited for our new boy to arrive. He was to be accompanied by his latest social worker, Phoebe Morris, who'd been allocated to him just six months ago after his previous social worker had gone on maternity leave. Christine had pre-warned me that Daniel might seem somewhat cool towards Phoebe as he'd really liked Amanda, his previous worker, and had taken it badly when she 'abandoned' him to have her baby. A fact of life, obviously, but also rather sad. Another relationship made and then over.

With a few minutes left to spare, I ran upstairs one last time to check on the newly refurbished room and was pleased to see that Mike must have been in before work and opened the window. It now smelled pleasingly fragrant – a mix of the great outdoors and my fabric conditioner – and since I set a lot of store by the calm, welcoming environment we brought kids into, I hoped it would help ease the transition. Every little helps, as some supermarket has it. And it was from up there that I saw a car approach and then park. This was it, then.

I ran back downstairs so I could wait smiling at the open door and reflected that this was our first placement ever to commence with such profound reservations. On our part, of course, but what of the lad who was now getting out of the car and going around the back to retrieve his luggage from the boot?

He was soon joined by his social worker, of whom, since she was on the pavement side, I now had a clearer view. Phoebe Morris was tall and very slender. She looked to be in her late thirties, with closely-cropped dark brown hair and startling bright pink glasses – almost as if a mask to hide behind. But even with them on, she still had the air of someone who'd been worn down by the job, increment by increment; barely smiling, she seemed the polar opposite of the cheerful girl who had brought Bella to us only the previous week. Or was it just having spent six months with Daniel as part of her caseload? Or had they had words on the journey? It was impossible to tell, of course, and I made a mental effort not to put two and two together. We had decided to give the lad a go, and go for it we must, even though the case file did make for such depressing reading. For now, I must take him as I found him in the hope of moving forwards.

Daniel's belongings all out of the boot, they now approached, with the lad, I was pleased to see, carrying the lion's share. 'Hi,' I said, smiling as they drew near. 'Do you need a hand with any of that?' I glanced at Daniel. 'You have a lot of stuff, I see.'

Daniel was exactly as he'd been described. Though it was difficult to see the resemblance between him and the cartoon version I'd seen on Bella's text, his colouring was familiar. Acne-scarred skin and almost black hair. He was also tall and thick-set, and with his well-established stubble, could easily pass for 18 or more. He grinned briefly at me. 'It's mainly all my gaming stuff,' he said. 'I could actually do with some new trackies and trainers and stuff.' He nodded towards his social worker as he stepped past me into the hall. 'She said you'd sort all that.'

She. The cat's mother. I arched my eyebrows as I looked at Phoebe for clarification, but she just shook her head and gave me a 'don't ask' look. There was clearly no love lost around there.

'Well, let's get inside with all this stuff,' I said. 'First things first, I think. I'll pop the kettle on and then we can get your things upstairs and you can see your room, Daniel. Sound like a plan?'

'Defo,' he said, then, at my invitation, came inside and headed straight up the stairs, taking them two at a time, as if he couldn't wait to get up there. And once in the bedroom, his delight at his new accommodation was obvious. 'Oh, my days!' he exclaimed, doing a 360-spin around to take it all in. Then he beamed at me: 'This is *sick*!'

A good start. His pleasure felt so genuine and also served to remind me that he'd come from a very different place. 'You like it then?' I asked him.

'I love it.'

'So why don't you start sorting your stuff out while Phoebe and I make a start on the paperwork? Unless you'd like to do that with us first?'

Breaking Point

'Nah, bruh,' he replied, dragging his large, battered suitcase up on to the bed. 'You guys have your meeting, I'm staying up here and setting up.'

'Okay,' I said, 'but before I go down, my name's Casey so no need for any bros, bruhs or fams. And while we're on the subject, do you prefer to be called Daniel, Dan or Danny?'

I had already decided to leave out the option of DJ, having no intention of using any nicknames, and was pleased to note that he seemed to understand.

'Cool,' he said. 'Dan's fine.' He smiled. 'No *way* is it Danny.'

I had no idea why he was so averse to that option but it didn't really matter. I headed down, buoyed up by such a positive first interaction.

Which was clearly on the mind of his social worker when I returned to her – me with a coffee and her with a glass of water.

'What do you think, then?' she asked as we sat down at the dining table. And I could tell by her body language that she was anxious to hear my thoughts. Which was fair enough. I guessed everything would be charged now with a level of anxiety. Would he step up to the challenge? Would we? Would it last?

Such a direct question, so early on, however, surprised me. Was she expecting me to have an answer to that already? To tell her that I'd decided there and then that Daniel was a keeper and there would be no need to worry? Or that I'd already decided we wanted him gone?

I smiled and took a sip of my coffee. 'I think,' I said slowly, 'that this is certainly a lad who is set in his ways and that he's used to being in control, and I also think at this point, despite his currently cheerful demeanour, that if I'm to look after him the way he should be looked after, then it's going to be a bumpy ride.'

Phoebe stared at me for a moment before answering. 'Wow!' she said, 'all that from 10 minutes?'

I shook my head. 'Not 10 minutes. I've had access to all his files, so I know what to expect. Plus,' I added with a smile, 'I have been doing this for a while now.'

She nodded thoughtfully. 'Well, I'm pleased to see that you're coming into this with your eyes wide open.'

'It was the only way to take it on,' I said. 'Plus, long, long experience with teenage boys has taught me to always look beneath the surface and I've become quite a good judge of character, I reckon. So, for all that he apparently seems happy to be here, I'm braced for a fair bit of initial conflict ...' I leaned forward to pick up the familiar, large, buff-coloured envelope. 'This is for me to read and sign?' I asked. Phoebe nodded. 'Anything new in there other than the case file I was sent?'

She shook her head as she picked up a pen and held it out for me. 'Nothing you won't already know,' she confirmed, 'but of course all his contacts etc. are listed in that and I believe your supervisor will be coming out sometime soon to go over a safe care plan.'

'So, looks like we're done, then?' she said, once I'd signed. She seemed keen to be off. She didn't want to go up and say goodbye to Daniel either, but I elected not to comment or ask for her own thoughts, as I had the impression I'd be putting her on the spot. No, let things lie and form my own first impressions. Having checked the paperwork reflected the terms we'd agreed, I placed it in my lockbox and went up to see how Daniel was getting on.

I was surprised to find him sitting at the desk, wearing a pair of large headphones, his PlayStation already all fired up. And he seemed to be gaming already, having obviously noticed the card with the Wi-Fi name and password that I had placed on the desk.

I called his name but he clearly couldn't hear me, so I walked across to him and waved my hand in front of his face, upon which he immediately pulled one side of the headphones down to his chin.

'Wassup?' he asked, but then he must have noticed the direction of my gaze, which was towards the bags and rucksacks still sitting untouched on the bed. 'I'm gonna sort that in a bit,' he said. 'I'm just in the middle of a tournament.'

'I can see that,' I said. He was obviously clear on his priorities. 'It's lunchtime though. Do you want a sandwich or something?'

'Nah, br ... I mean, Casey. Thanks, but I had a Maccy D's on the way over.'

'Okay,' I said, happy that he'd readjusted how he addressed me. I then pointed to the bed. 'But make sure you put all your clothes and things away before teatime, please, Dan. And I'll be downstairs if you want to join me, or if you need anything.'

Daniel's response to this was just a nod before the headphones were rearranged and the furious clicking of the controller began again. I sighed and closed the door behind me, and as I went back down the stairs, a familiar sense of gloom couldn't help but settle. Teenage boys and gaming ... I knew studies proved that it was not, for the most part, harmful. And, yes, I knew all about the benefits to their hand-to-eye co-ordination and problem-solving skills. But it was wearing, nevertheless, to have a machine, plus the internet – a third, and demanding 'person' – in our relationship. Still, I told myself, at least this was the silver lining of him being equipped with headphones, so I didn't have to listen to the inevitable noise. Why, though, did this not-at-all-unusual exchange leave me feeling a bit discomfited? The boy was clearly comfortable in his own room, keeping himself busy – much as he might have been for years in the children's home. I could get along with whatever I wanted to do downstairs – catch up with TV, do a bit of reading, gardening, anything really.

Stop it, Casey, I told myself. *When do you actually do any of that stuff?* Instead, I caught up with a few phone calls to the family and then decided it was high time I stopped putting off cleaning and defrosting the freezer, which meant pulling out all the almost-empty bags of mixed peppers, onions and vegetables I'd been hoarding for months, sure I'd come up with an inventive recipe that would make use of them all, plus free up that much-needed space once I was done.

Almost before I knew it, I'd done exactly that; prepared and made meatballs and a delicious pasta sauce, all from scratch, that did indeed call for quite a lot of my leftover freezer stock. I was just shaving some Parmesan onto the finished meal when Mike got in from work. He glanced around the room and kitchen and gave me a puzzled look.

'Where is he, then?'

'Remember how Sammy spent all his time in his room?' I asked. Sammy, the last boy we'd had staying with us, had also been something of a recluse. 'Well, it looks as if Dan might be cut from the same cloth. I showed him his room when he arrived and he's not emerged since. I've been up and down those stairs like I'm in training for a marathon, but nope, he'd rather just stay up there. Far as I can tell, he hasn't yet come off his bloody PlayStation.'

'Where you going with that?' Mike asked as he watched me portion some tea out and then set off towards the hall with it.

'Well,' I said, 'if the mountain won't come to Mohammed ...'

'No, Casey, don't do that,' said Mike, taking the plate from me. 'That would be setting an unhealthy precedent. Let me try and coax him down here first.'

I conceded and then listened at the bottom of the stairs as Mike went to introduce himself to Daniel. I heard a bit of mumbling and then Mike's voice, which carried, saying, 'Come on then, lad. Casey's made us a lovely tea. It'll only take you 10 minutes then you can go back to hibernation if you must.'

There was a bit of clattering then and, very soon after, the pair of them came down the stairs. Not that it looked as though our new house guest had come willingly. He seemed sullen and there was a tic in Mike's jaw. Still, he'd achieved what he'd set out to do and seemed determined to make things light and normal. 'Smells lovely, that does, Case,' he said as he sat down. 'Sit yourself down, lad,' he added, pointing to the chair opposite. 'You're going to love this, it's Casey's secret recipe.'

'Yes,' I said, smiling, 'it's called *hotchpotch à la freezer*.'

Which produced precisely nothing by way of acknowledgement. Indeed, for the next 10 minutes, while we ate, all our conversational parries produced little more than the odd grunt. We ended up finishing in silence and after Daniel, his plate clean, politely asked if it was okay to go back upstairs, I couldn't help but sigh at the prospect of this being our new normal.

'Though I'm sure it'll get less awkward,' I said to Mike. 'He doesn't know us yet, does he? And given that he wasn't even pushing for this move, he's bound to be a bit off with us at first.'

'I agree,' Mike conceded. 'And it's not like he's even being "off" particularly – we just play second fiddle to that kit up there. And we may as well make the most of it for a bit. Let him take his few days to settle in however he chooses, at least until they sort out some form of education or whatever, and in the meantime, we can just enjoy the peace and quiet.'

Mike was echoing my own thoughts and I knew I should try to relax, but I couldn't shake the unsettling feeling I had of being trapped. There wasn't any obvious reason to feel that way – I mean, the boy was old enough to be left if I needed to go to the shops or anything like that – but I knew better than to ignore my own nagging doubts.

'You're right,' I said, rather than give vent to my worries. 'You go have your shower and I'll do the washing-up and then we'll sit down and find a decent movie or something. Our Riley keeps banging on about us never watching *Game of Thrones*. Why don't we give that a try?'

Mike was right. Our daughter Riley had been going on about it endlessly. She and her partner David were obsessed with it. So that's what we did on Daniel's first night with us. He played shoot-'em-up upstairs and we watched about four episodes of the most gruesome yet addictive series I'd ever seen. In fact, it was midnight before we tore ourselves away from the TV and that was only because Mike needed to get some sleep to be up early for work.

Once upstairs, I listened discreetly outside of Daniel's room, but all was quiet and within about half an hour, I was fast asleep, knowing that I'd probably feel less unsettled come the morning.

The morning, however, came earlier than I'd expected. It was exactly 4 a.m. when I realised that my doubts about Daniel were indeed justified as I was woken up with a start by the sound of shouting and swearing. Fearing Mike would wake too and lose his precious last couple of hours, I leapt out of bed and ran to where the racket was coming from: Daniel's room, of course. I rapped on the door.

Unsurprisingly, my knocks went unheard and the shouting and swearing continued. Indeed, it seemed to be ramping up in volume. So, I opened the door and stepped inside, to see Daniel at the desk, headphones on, seemingly having the time of his life as he continued to shout at the screen.

'Go on, you fucking pussy boy! Fuck you, bruh!'

To say I was fuming was something of an understatement. Since he hadn't even noticed that I'd entered the room, I marched straight across and, disregarding any thought that I might startle him, pulled one headphone away from his ear.

'Dan!' I shouted. 'What the hell are you doing at this time of the morning? And you can stop using that language in this house, right now.'

'What the actual fuck?' he shouted, glaring up at me. 'Can't you see I'm in the middle of something?'

'Quit the swearing,' I repeated, as evenly as I could

Breaking Point

muster. 'And I really don't care what you're in the middle of. It's the middle of the night and in this house, that means it's time for sleeping, not gaming, so tell whoever that is that you'll speak to them tomorrow.'

'Are you mad, woman?' Daniel said. 'Everyone's online at this time of night, innit? I sleep in the day when it's quiet.'

Unbelievably, he then slipped his headphones back on and turned back to his screen. 'Yo, bro, I'm back,' he said, laughing. He then resumed furiously operating the control pad with his thumbs.

I stared at the scene before me and replayed what had just happened in my head. There was clearly only one thing to do here: I walked out and closed the door, then calmly walked downstairs into the living room, where I switched off the internet. I waited, as I knew it would take a minute or two to have the desired effect. It did. I then heard an almighty bang and another bout of – this time – angry swearing.

'You fucking bitch! Fuck you! Fuck *both* of you!'

I walked back upstairs, clutching the Wi-Fi hub, by now physically shaking. I knew I dare not leave it downstairs just in case Daniel decided he'd go switch it back on himself. Also, I knew I must go back into his bedroom – to leave this now would set another undesirable precedent. All I needed to do though was respond to what he'd said, have the last word. To assert my authority. So, I didn't knock this time, I just opened the door.

I was surprised to see that his TV was off and less so to see both controller and headphones on the floor, where he had obviously thrown them. Daniel himself was curled up in bed with his back to me, so he clearly wasn't up for a fight. A confrontation at this point therefore wasn't necessary, thank goodness, and would only serve to escalate a potentially volatile situation. 'Good night, Dan,' I told him. 'We'll discuss rules around Wi-Fi in the morning.'

A barely audible 'fuck you' was all that followed.

It was all over in minutes and no huge confrontation had ensued, so as I climbed back into bed, grateful that Mike had slept through it, I knew I should have felt that, okay, this was probably par for the course. I had, after all, dealt with many stroppy, aggressive teenagers in my time, each with their own set of challenges. In the big scheme of things this altercation was really no biggie yet the unease persisted. This felt, somehow, different. I wasn't sure why, because rationally it wasn't. But it settled in my mind and demanded to be heard.

Had we just made a terrible mistake?

Chapter 4

With Mike having, thankfully, missed all the previous night's drama, when he brought my coffee up the next morning, I sat up in bed and told him all about what had happened.

'You should have woken me up,' he said, his face set in a tight expression. 'Did he try to intimidate you?'

I thought for a moment before answering. Had he? No, not really. Just been defiant and, once thwarted in his gaming, had thrown his toys – literally – out of his pram. I shook my head. 'No, at least I don't think his intention was to intimidate. To be honest, I think he was just like on a high. Not on an actual high,' I clarified. 'Just the usual gaming thing – hyper-focussed. It was like he was in a whole other realm, you know? He seemed surprised that I was even there at first. You know what it's like; completely immersed in his alternate reality.'

Mike shook his head. 'Well, unfortunately, he lives in the real world,' he said as he made to leave for work.

'Which means abiding by our house rules around times he can do his gaming. And if it means unplugging his access to the internet, then that's what will happen until he learns.'

After Mike left, I checked the time: it was still only a little after seven. And my hunch was that Daniel would be asleep for a good while yet, giving me time to shower and eat breakfast before dealing with my first task of the day, which was to phone the children's home as soon as they opened their reception. Despite all of the information I'd already received about Daniel, I'd not really had a snapshot of his daily routines – if indeed he had any – and I also had questions I needed answering.

My second task, as I'd already decided after our small hours' confrontation, would be to wake him up as soon as I'd finished my call, whether he liked it or not. I suspected he would be none too keen, but, for all of our sakes – his included – I had to at least try to put some structure in place so that Daniel would be less inclined to stay up all night gaming.

At 9 a.m. sharp, I was put through to the children's home manager, a lady called June Hicken, and introduced myself before telling her what had happened the night before.

'Is this normal behaviour for Dan?' I asked, 'or do you think it might have been that he couldn't sleep due to the fact that he'd been moved yesterday?'

'Oh, it's completely normal,' June said with a slight chuckle in her voice. 'He's a bit of a night owl is our

Breaking Point

Deejay, I'm afraid. Unsurprising though really, when you consider his situation here.'

'I don't understand,' I said, feeling a little confused. 'Why would his situation there mean that he was up all night, gaming?'

I think I must have got her back up a bit with that, because when she spoke next, she definitely did not have a chuckle in her voice.

'Well, it's not like we could simply turn the WI-Fi off here, is it? The night staff need it, for a start, and as for trying to stop him playing, that wasn't an option either. Our staff can't be going in and physically wrestling devices away from the kids – some of them, anyway, because they can get pretty violent – and Deejay would definitely have put up a fight if they tried it with him – so it was much easier to leave him to it,' she added briskly. 'It wasn't as if it affected anyone else.'

Much easier for them, I thought crossly. How about the affect it had on him? Did that not matter? My back was up now too and I couldn't help the sarcasm that had found its way into my tone.

'So, if he was allowed to game all night, what did he do during the day, then? Just sleep?'

'Look,' June answered, 'you have to remember that when Deejay was placed with us, he was only 12. All the other kids here at the time were much older, and despite his young street cred, he was terrified. Terrified of all of them. He wouldn't go in the common areas, where they all hung out – he'd just lock himself away and shut out all the chaos with his headphones and gaming. He played through the night, and slept his days away, unless there were activities that he wanted to go on, such as days out to theme parks or climbing centres. He used to like those,' she finished, sounding almost wistful – for the pre-teen he used to be and no longer was? But hormones happened, to all children. It was a wholly natural process. Yet it sounded almost as if, as soon as Daniel had hit puberty, it hadn't been about boundaries being rigorously reinforced, more that the stroppier he got, the more the staff had backed off. As if the boundaries – those important brakes on adolescent excesses – had simply gone.

'Right,' I said, trying my best to tamp down my growing annoyance. Because it now seemed so clear. Daniel had simply been contained for the last three years; given room and board, and the freedom to do exactly as he pleased, rather than being looked after properly. 'So, his drug dealing, when did he find the time to do that? Through the night as well?'

June sounded slightly embarrassed now and was clearly not deaf to my insinuations. 'I'm sorry, Mrs Watson,' she said, 'but we are really, really stretched here and have been for a long time. The budget cuts year after year have meant that the staff we employ at night … well, although they have qualifications, they're the very minimum required and so their duties are very different to the day staff. There are only two sleepover employees and there's no way they can constantly keep a check on all the kids. They just couldn't do it. Often by the time they're aware of a child not being back in for curfew, it's too late – they're long gone.'

I did sympathise with her predicament, but it still angered me that the most vulnerable in our society often appear to be the most overlooked.

'I get that,' I said, 'and then I guess it's the same old story – the Emergency Duty Team [EDT] and the police are informed, the police make a half-hearted effort to round them up, but more often than not, they can't be found and then the kids simply turn up again when they're hungry?' I'd experienced and heard about this scenario more times than I cared to think about.

'Exactly that, I'm afraid,' June said, 'and our hands are tied. It's so frustrating because it makes us feel –well, me, anyway – that the job we originally signed up for, to properly care for these children and give them a fighting chance, no longer exists. It's all about containment these days and meeting minimum standards. Keep them fed, keep them hydrated, give them somewhere to sleep, and supply an endless stream of spending money. Yes, it ticks all the right boxes, but where's the nurture? The love? It's no wonder we struggle to keep our staff long term.'

I now felt bad for doubting this manager's sincerity. In reality, she simply felt the way we often did: restricted by budgets, red tape and a system that was constantly being squeezed of its humanity. Even the most resilient of carers, in any capacity, must be affected by the whole thing and I knew that, at least for foster carers, the burnout rate was increasing by the month. Couples were leaving almost weekly, citing that it was simply too much to have to deal with. But at least they had their families in situ and worked from the comfort of their own homes. The staff and management at children's homes must sometimes dread going into work, for fear of what they might be confronted with.

'It's not good, is it?' I agreed, all confrontation on my own part now forgotten. We were both on the same team and it didn't help any of us if we were being adversarial with one another. I also felt chastened, and guilty. Like all of us, June was doing her best and was probably fielding criticism all the time. 'And we both know the effect on these kids is long-lasting. Little wonder they come to foster families with the expectation that they will be left to their own devices and without respect for either people or rules – I just wish I knew what the solution is.'

'There isn't one,' she said flatly. 'Not a fast fix one anyway. Not unless the government suddenly decides that children really are our future and invest heavily in their well-being, so all we can do is just plod on and try our best to make a difference. Truth is, when a family is found for one of our children, I thank God, I really do. And just pray that they are going to a loving home and will at last get to see what stability and normality look like. Though I recognise,' she added, making me feel even worse, 'that they're not coming to you from the best place, much as I wish it were different. Kids like Deejay … well, I know you're going to have your work cut out with that lad. But I can't be sorry he's with you. Not because I'm glad to be shot of a kid who's hard to manage, but because in agreeing to take on the challenge, you're at least throwing him a lifeline. And I guess all we can do is hope he has the sense to grab it.'

To which all I could do was apologise for my tone earlier and reassure her that I understood where she was coming from. And she was right of course: all any of us could do was plod on, as she'd put it. Plod on and desperately hope that we could manage to make a positive impact on a disillusioned, abandoned child. The baton had been passed. Now it was time for me to pick it up.

Chapter 5

Rome wasn't built in a day. Such a clichéd old saying, but five days in with Daniel and I had made it my mantra. I sighed wearily as I walked up the stairs towards his bedroom. It was 10 a.m., on a lovely bright early autumn morning, and for the fifth time, exactly as per the plan I had settled on, my first job was to do everything in my power to get him to wake up and see it. No, not see it in the sense of the boy gambolling around in the back garden, admiring Mike's dahlias – I wasn't in the habit of performing miracles – but at least *compos mentis* and out of bed before noon.

I stopped on the landing and took a deep breath before knocking at his bedroom door – not because I was nervous about the coming confrontation, because that was a given, but out of existential weariness because I had no reason to believe that this morning was going to be any different to the previous ones.

When I got no reply, I did some internal self-talking – *straighten up, Casey, you're the one in charge, you can do this*, and so on – before turning the door handle and walking in.

'Dan!' I called out brightly as I walked towards his bed. As usual, he had his back to me and the duvet clutched tightly around his body. I placed a hand on his shoulder and shook him gently.

'It's time to get up, Dan,' I said, still very brightly. 'The Wi-Fi is back on if you want to go online, or you can come downstairs for some breakfast.'

He didn't open his eyes, much less move any part of his body. Just issued a 'Fuck my life! Why can't you just leave me the fuck alone?'

So far so same as the previous two mornings. 'I'm sorry, Dan, but the answer's no. That's not an option and you know it. We had this conversation yesterday and the day before. We also spoke about you not using that language in this house. Now, come on,' I finished, less brightly, '*move* yourself.'

Daniel opened his eyes, finally, and twisted his head around so he could glare at me properly. '*Why*, though?' he whined. 'Why can't you just let me sleep? I'm *tired*, okay?'

As per the plan, I kept my voice low and even. 'Dan, as you well know, you should be in education at your age, and if you were, then you'd have to be up every weekday and far earlier than this, so …'

'But I'm *not*, am I?' he barked before turning back to the wall and pulling the duvet up over his head. 'And you're doing everything you can to ruin my fucking *life*. Can you leave, please? I need the toilet. And I'm naked.'

It was almost as if an idea had suddenly bloomed in his brain. Because he rolled back over now, towards me, and clutched a wodge of the duvet, staring pointedly at me, with a half-smile on his face, as if daring me to stay and watch as he whipped it away. Was this one of his tools to intimidate the young staff at the children's home? If so, on this occasion, he'd miscalculated. Because I stayed where I was, contemplating pointing out that there was nothing under the duvet I hadn't seen many, many times before.

I didn't, though. I stood my ground and simply dared him with my smile. 'I'll be back up in half an hour,' I said, after a long moment passed. 'To make sure you are awake and out of bed. I'll bring some cereal or toast. Any preference. Or even both?'

'Nothing,' he snapped back. 'I don't want any food, I just want to take a piss. *Okay*?'

I left him to it, then, teeth gritted, and went back downstairs. His swearing was really beginning to get on my nerves now, but logically I knew I could only tackle one problem at a time and the most important, in my opinion, was to establish a pattern that would enable Daniel to sleep through the night and remain awake throughout the day. Not an easy task for somebody who had spent possibly years doing exactly the opposite and I had to acknowledge that while pressing on, trying to change it. I also had to acknowledge that this current pattern wasn't

Breaking Point

really his fault at all, so despite my own frustrations, I had to just disregard his anger and bad language as much as I could while continuing to firmly push my own agenda. Because, bottom line, this first hurdle was a relatively simple business. He wanted to sleep the day away, I wanted him awake. If we couldn't crack that, we were heading nowhere. But if we *did* ... Well, who knew how many miracles we might accomplish?

Back in the kitchen I made breakfast for him almost on autopilot, reflecting that getting Daniel either up, or to go to sleep, now bookended my every day. Because it had been the same kind of battle every evening, as well. The Wi-Fi was turned off at 11.30 p.m. and the hub brought to our bedroom. By Mike, though, as he'd opted to do the night-time confrontation, so I didn't have to deal with Daniel's anger for a second time. Though, from the sanctuary of our bed, I could still, of course, hear it. And each time, I would know exactly when his connection was lost, due to the stream of loud expletives and the similarly loud bang that followed as something was furiously thrown.

'Just let him do it, Casey,' Mike had said on the second night. 'It's his own headset and control pad he's throwing around. He's not stupid – he surely knows that if he breaks them, he won't be able to play and it's as simple as that, because we definitely won't be replacing them if he does.'

It was becoming a little like Groundhog Day, the first confrontation taking place at 10 a.m. sharp, then some breakfast delivered, whether he wanted it or not, then I'd go up half an hour later to find Dan fast asleep again and enjoy another torrent of abuse when I tried to wake him. It was usually after midday by the time I would finally have him get out of bed. Or, rather, leap out of bed, because by now, he would be in a rage. Which was intimidating to watch and listen to, but I had to stand firm. Keep my voice low and even, keep restating my position, use repetitive words, hammer home what I needed from him and thus retain a measure of control. *Please don't shout. Calm down, please, Dan. Are you hungry? Would you like a drink?* All go-to questions I would use to try and restore order, as well as opening the curtains, opening a window, opening a conversation about the weather and then, whatever his response, or more often, lack of, I would turn around and go back downstairs, where, just as I knew I'd be doing later on *this* day, I'd make more food – a sandwich, a pizza, or some instant noodles – then add some snacks, make up another tray, then take it all straight back up to his bedroom.

Still, at least I was beginning to learn *something* about him. Though he'd not come to us with the usual list of food preferences, I was familiarising myself with them anyway, based on what had been eaten or left untouched on the trays.

And today was proving no different. I took the tray up, he ignored it, then I got on with some housework and by the time I returned and 'abused' him – his words

– for a second time, I was able to note that he liked peanut butter, but not Marmite, and that orange juice was obviously undrinkable.

And so the morning passed by, as had all the previous mornings, with oases of normality punctuated by arguments, then lunch – mine a sandwich in the kitchen, and Daniel's his usual tray – and finally, a boy at least awake, if not always dressed. Though why would he dress? He rarely ever seemed to want to leave his bedroom – and, when it came to teenagers, if they had no interest in leaving their bedrooms, and no school to go to, as was the case with Daniel, it was almost impossible to winkle them out.

But today, to my delight, there was a breakthrough. I don't know what prompted it, but, at around 2 p.m., while I was scrolling through my vast cache of holiday photos, Daniel appeared in the kitchen, holding his tray, and also dressed.

I watched without comment as he took the tray around and behind me to place it by the sink. Then, since he made no move to leave again – he was now swilling out a glass and filling it with water from the tap – I swivelled round on the bar stool I was perching on and thanked him.

'But tell me,' I continued, keen to seize this opportunity, 'don't you get bored being stuck up there, just gaming all day?'

'No, not really,' he said. Then seemed to give the matter further thought. 'I mean, it's a bit shit through the day,' he added, ''cos, like, hardly any of my mates are online.'

While he downed some more water, I resisted the urge to point out that might be because everyone else was in school, but that wouldn't have been helpful; he surely knew that already. So instead, I nodded. 'So, when do they all start coming on then?'

'Around seven,' he supplied. 'But then I don't get long proper gaming – in tournaments and stuff – 'cos you guys turn everything off.' He lowered his gaze. 'That's what gets me so mad.'

'Yes,' I said, taking his cue and going to fill the kettle – that way I wouldn't be looking at him. 'You're mad because it's what you've been used to doing. I get that. But it's not normal for someone your age to be up all night and sleeping all day. You must know that, Dan,' I finished mildly.

'Oh, my days,' he said. 'You think that? There's *loads* of people do that. All my mates, for one. It's *so* normal.'

'Seriously, Dan? At *your* age? Do your mates go to school then?'

He shook his head. 'No, 'course not – they're all older.' Now he looked at me. 'Can't you start leaving the Wi-Fi on till half twelve? I mean, really. *Just* till half twelve? Can't you? *Please*?'

Was this why he'd come down? To try a different tactic? If so, I could at least chalk up a small win, I supposed. He'd obviously given thought to the fact that the shouting and dogged defiance wasn't working. But this wouldn't either. It couldn't, because it mustn't. We'd set the rule, and the boundary, and now we absolutely had to stick to it. Which meant this conversation could soon turn into an argument.

I had to think on my feet. 'Could you pass me the milk?' I asked, pointing towards the fridge. 'And while you're at it, if you see anything in there you fancy for tea, let me know. I'm struggling to think of what to make today.' I smiled. 'Perhaps you can be the decider for a change.'

If he was confused by my heading off on this unexpected tangent, he clearly wasn't about to say so. Perhaps he'd decided not to push things – at least not yet. Instead, he duly opened the fridge, passed the carton of milk to me and then, as instructed, peered inside and started rummaging.

'There's mince here,' he said, finally. 'Do you know how to make a curry? I like curry,' he added, shutting the door again.

It was the first piece of unsolicited concrete information that he'd given me. 'Absolutely I can,' I assured him. 'I make a mean curry. Usually with chicken, to be fair, but I can have a go with mince.'

'It's called Keema,' Dan said. 'My uncle's ex-girlfriend used to make it for me sometimes. It's really spicy, proper hot.'

'I'm not sure "proper hot" is going to work for us, to be honest. Will "quite hot" do? You can always add your own extra chilli.'

'No, it's cool,' he said. 'I mean, not cool, but not too hot's cool, yeah? But, listen, you know, about the Wi-Fi. How about if I—'

'How about,' I said, my mind having been whirring, 'you and I strike a deal?'

'A deal?' he asked, his eyes narrowing in suspicion now. 'What kind of deal?'

'As in how about I ask my fostering boss if she can get you into some part-time education – you know, to fill at least a few of those days up a bit – and on the days you don't have it, we allow you to play later and have a lie-in the next day? What about that?'

It seemed to take a while for Daniel to process what I was suggesting. Then he shook his head. 'Not going to happen. They won't let me. I've been permanently excluded from two schools for fighting, there's only units left for me and they're filled with bad kids. Half them kids are from the same home I was in and they hate me. Besides, there's no way I'd be able to go every day from now till I can leave. No way!' He shook his head again. 'I couldn't do it.'

It was a long speech and felt like another small win. 'Okay,' I said, 'I hear you. But what if it *were* possible to get you in somewhere, but not the place you're on about? What if we could get you just a couple of days a week somewhere else? Somewhere nicer? Would you be prepared to give it a try?'

There was another long pause while he chewed my idea over and I had no idea how he was going to respond. After all, he'd come from a place where no one made him go to school, and no one seemed to object to his nocturnal lifestyle. What I was proposing was never going to take him back to that level of freedom so why on earth would he agree to it? But perhaps five days under our roof had brought it home to Daniel that his new reality was exactly that – his situation in the real world. It was impossible to know whether he found any comfort or solace in living in a family home as opposed to a children's home, but he must, I reckoned, have accepted that this was how life was going to be now, at least until he was 16 (and in my view, ideally 18) because, finally, he shrugged.

'I s'pose you can try,' he offered.

'And you'll do it? If I can get that?'

He smiled slightly. 'You probs won't. But yeah, if you do. But you swear down I'll get later Wi-Fi if I do?'

'On the days when you don't have to get up, yes, as I said. And at weekends, as we've already agreed. I'll speak to Mike tonight and then I'll call my social worker in the morning, but I already know they'll both be onboard. But Dan,' I said, passing him the milk carton back. 'You know the rules in this house, love, and if you do start back in education, you've got to keep your end of the bargain. If you refuse to get up and actually *go* to what we've fixed up, then our deal is off, okay?'

'Sound,' he said, as he put the milk back in the fridge for me. 'I'm off back upstairs, but don't be getting me nowhere that I have to do five days a week at, 'cos I'm not down for that level of shit.'

The bad language still being a problem for another day, I merely nodded and said 'noted'. And after he'd gone back upstairs, I sat back down with my coffee to think. That unexpected encounter had gone rather well, I decided. Certainly, much better than I would have imagined. Everyone had been so clear that Daniel had refused to engage with any form of education, yet the way he was telling it, it wasn't even in his hands. Or perhaps he was just trying to play me. It was one thing to agree to it, quite another to actually do it. But since the deal was that he had to do it *before* any change to the rules around the Wi-Fi, I didn't see how he could think that. I just hoped Mike would be okay with the idea. He might feel differently about trading the one thing for the other – and perhaps he was right. Perhaps Daniel should accept some form of schooling in any case, if he was to stay with us, with no bartering or bribery involved. But Mike was also a pragmatist – I was sure he'd be fine.

Getting that bit of education, though – that was a different matter. With places for previously excluded kids like Daniel so scarce, I might find myself struggling there. This would be no easy task and once I'd had the go-ahead from Christine, my supervisor, I'd have to make a very strong case for him. But I was determined that I'd cut through any red tape they tried to wrap me up in, no matter how fiercely I'd need to advocate for him. And, if it came to it, I did at least have an ace up my sleeve: they knew where we stood. If I faced a lot of pushback, I'd use it. I would simply tell them no education, no placement.

But writing that compelling email was a job for next week. Right now, I had a more pressing job to do. Google how to make Daniel his Keema curry …

Chapter 6

Since we'd started fostering all those years ago, Mike and I had cared for children of all ages. We'd also started out actively embracing the bigger challenges; we'd been specifically trained for a now-defunct fostering programme, taking on kids that were often so psychologically challenged that lots of other foster families wouldn't. And we were good at it – full of energy and passion for what we did. My former career, as head of a behaviour unit at a large comprehensive school, had helped enormously. I'd already seen so much, and been around so many damaged, troubled teenagers, that there was really very little a child could do that could faze me. We'd had all kinds of kids come to us, and from all sorts of backgrounds, from little ones – innocents so young, they had no idea that they had been sexually abused – to older kids who'd already seen and experienced the sort of horrors that no child should ever, ever have to. And, for the most part, with one or two painful exceptions, we believed we had at least made some positive difference to their lives, which was why so many of our former foster kids, most now adults themselves, still kept in touch with us. So, this unexpected glimpse into the possibility that we might just be able to do the same with Daniel had kept me buoyed up for the rest of that afternoon. Plus, for the first time in all the days he'd been with us, he came down from his room to join us for his Keema curry (very nice, as it turned out) and though conversation was difficult, in the inevitable getting-blood-out-of-a-stone manner, he at least sat at the dining table for a full 20 minutes and was even animated, briefly, when Mike steered the chat towards football, a subject it turned out he knew quite a bit about.

As I'd expected, however, as soon as the food was finished, Daniel hot-footed it straight back to his bedroom. But this at least allowed us space to discuss the coming week, even if it could, at this stage, only be hypothetical. I'd also given more thought to the terms of our 'deal' and come up with what I thought was a reasonable idea.

'I've been thinking,' I said to Mike, once we were settled on the sofa and I'd run the events of the afternoon past him properly, 'this whole Wi-Fi switch-off thing and the school situation ...'

'*If* we get it,' he pointed out. 'That's no way a given.'

'Except it is. The more I think about it, the more it seems to me that we have to make it a red line. No schooling, the placement ends. We stick to our guns. Because if they can't find any sort of education provision for him, I don't see how we carry on anyway. Him just mouldering away up there, like a hermit, week after week, month after month – that's got to be the very definition of being "not in his best interests". It might be acceptable – just – in an overstretched children's home, but in *our* home? No way! They surely must understand that. Because what's the point of him even being here if we're doing nothing to try and help get him back on track, especially when there are so many kids out there who could really benefit from being fostered? No, I'm pretty sure they'll find somewhere that'll take him.'

'*If* he'll actually go, when it comes to it,' Mike observed.

'Which brings me to my point. He's agreed to going, so we have to take him at his word, don't we? Which got me thinking. I know the agreement was that this whole "deal" we've brokered will start only once some sort of school provision is fixed up and he's actually doing it, but I was thinking, maybe we should throw the ball in his court before that.'

'In what way? I'm not sure I get your meaning.'

'In that we place our trust in him, throw a bit of goodwill in his direction. I mean, we're coming from a place of such negativity where Dan is concerned. And quite reasonably, obviously, because pretty much everything we've heard about him so far has been negative – that's why we are where we are. But it feels like we made a small breakthrough this afternoon, so how about we flip things and accentuate the positive?'

Mike grinned. 'Blimey! Have you swallowed a psychology textbook or something, or just been listening to showtunes?'

'No, *listen*,' I said, giving him a shoulder bump, as he broke into song. 'It just occurred to me that this is a lad who's so used to people thinking the worst of him that proving them right is almost a knee-jerk reaction. How about we counteract that by letting him know that we *do* have faith in him? That we *do* trust him to uphold his end of the bargain? He says he'll engage with education again, so let's let him know that we believe him. Let him do his late-night gaming this weekend – give him that little bit of slack – kind of as a down payment on him doing what he'd agreed to once we get something in place. Show him some positivity, essentially. What do you think?'

'Honestly? I think you're being a bit over-optimistic. And even if we do get some kind of workable schedule in place, how is this whole thing going to work logistically? Are we meant to set ourselves an alarm at 2 a.m. or something, so one of us can come down and switch off the Wi-Fi? Or were you thinking we'd just leave it on all night at weekends and whichever other nights he doesn't have to be up early?'

To be honest, I hadn't thought that far ahead. At the time I'd just been happy that Dan was up for going back to school. At a price of course, but still … 'I didn't say anything to him about times,' I admitted, 'but honestly, Mike, I think that even if we just leave it on all night, he'll go to sleep when he's tired, regardless, and if we allow him to sleep later the following day, but not too much later, then I think our lives will be a lot less stressful and at least he'll be back in education, which is no small feat.'

'So, when do you propose we start this thing? Tonight? I mean, I get your point about making this all about us putting our trust in him, but to me it still feels a little like we've caved in. And after the week we've had with him, won't he just be getting the message that if he kicks off enough, we'll give in to him?'

'No, that's my whole point. We make it really clear that we're doing this *precisely* because he's agreed to accept our position – that having those privileges is dependent on him going back to school. As long as he understands that, I think it's workable. And if, come next week, he doesn't play ball, then we're no worse off – just back where we started. No education, no placement.'

'Well, if that's the way you want to play it, I'm happy to play along. So just for the weekend, for now, yes?'

'Yes, I'll explain that it's just for tonight and tomorrow, and then on Sunday night it will go off as usual, all as if he had to get up for school.'

'Okay, Case,' said Mike. 'As I said, we'll do it your way, but let's see if he's as obliging as you are when it comes to Sunday night. You might be right, but I wouldn't bet my life on it, that's for sure. And when you tell him, make sure you let him know that after 11 p.m., we best not hear him arguing online, otherwise I'll be making an addition to the deal. His headphones and mic will be removed before we go to bed as well. Make sure he understands that.'

Since the last thing I wanted was to be disturbed from my sleep in the early hours, weekend or not, I agreed. And when I went upstairs to tell Daniel what we'd decided, his response reassured me that I'd made a good plan. He seemed genuinely surprised and genuinely grateful. There wasn't a trace of him seeming smug – as if he'd cleverly got one over us – and I have a good nose for such things. He was also accepting of Mike's extra proviso of no shouting or swearing; that if he woke us up during the night, the deal was off.

'Okay, and I swear down you won't hear me,' he promised. 'But you will have to let me know when it's 11, 'cos I lose track of time. I'll turn my mic off when you let me know and I'll just use my keyboard if I need to talk to anyone. It's a pisstake typing it all out, but I'll do it.'

I sighed at his delightful choice of language again. 'I presume you meant to say "a pain in the butt"?'

He nodded sheepishly, which made me smile. It was good to see him looking shamefaced. Proof indeed that at least some things *were* getting through.

And, on Friday night and Saturday night, the plan worked. On both evenings, Mike knocked on Daniel's bedroom door at 11 and opened it to be sure he'd been seen and heard. He reminded Daniel that it was night-time now and we didn't expect to be woken, and he duly 'swore down' that we wouldn't be. And we weren't. But as every Roman architect probably knew very well, ambitious projects invariably involve hiccups.

Our hiccup happened on Sunday night. With Monday being a work day, and, potentially, soon a school day, we'd turned the Wi-Fi off at ten thirty though, in the spirit of trust and positivity we'd opted for, we had elected not to take the router up to bed with us. And all was well, until the middle of the night, when I woke with a start. I then realised that Mike, whose alarm was due to go off at 5.30, was no longer in bed.

I sat up, threw the duvet off and swung my legs out of bed, aware now that I could hear my husband's raised voice, coming from just beyond the partially open bedroom door. I was surprised at the tone, which was, for Mike, unusually raised and clearly agitated.

'No, Dan, I'm telling *you*,' he said. 'I pay the bills in this house, mate, including the internet, and until you learn to have a bit more respect, this is what will happen and no amount of smashing things up will entice me to turn it back on. You broke the deal, mate, not me.'

I then heard Daniel's bedroom door being closed loudly and his muffled voice yelling back, '*Fuck* you! And fuck going to school as well, you fat bastard!'

Two things were immediately apparent. That Daniel must have sneaked downstairs and turned the Wi-Fi back on – that trust we'd placed in him now completely broken, I thought miserably – and that the lad took in more than we knew. Mike was far from being fat, but he was troubled by his recent weight gain. Earlier that evening, while the three of us had been having one of our awkward dinners, he had commented on the fact that he reckoned he'd put on half a stone since injuring his knee, mostly because he couldn't do so much manual stuff at work, or play football. The fact that Daniel had stored that away and brought it out when he had really made my blood boil. Also, work … I checked my phone, it was approaching three thirty.

'I'm bloody fuming,' Mike hissed, when he returned to the bedroom, the Wi-Fi router now in his hands. 'You should have heard the carry-on in there. He was yelling at the top of his voice – it's a wonder he didn't wake the entire street! Then the little sod tried telling me to get out and when I told him the Wi-Fi was going off, he even laughed at me!'

'I'm so sorry, love,' I said, nestling close to him once he'd got back into bed. 'And you are *not* fat, far from it – if that's any consolation.'

'Not really,' Mike said. 'Look at the bloody time, love! I'm going to be knackered at work tomorrow and there's no way I'm going to be able to get back to sleep now. I just can't get over how bloody brazen he is. He just doesn't care at all. Oh, and he's now saying he isn't going to go to school either. Well,' he huffed, 'we shall see about *that*.'

'How about I pop the TV on quietly?' I suggested. 'That always helps you drift off. And remember, I mean it. He *will* be going to school. Either that or *he* goes. End of. We're getting too bloody old for this kind of lark.'

'Speak for yourself,' Mike muttered.

Thankfully, my poor husband quickly drifted back off to sleep, but I lay there for at least another hour, playing out conversations in my mind – the ones I needed to have with both the social worker and Christine. This placement was a rolling, month-by-month commitment, but at this rate I was beginning to think we might not even last the first fortnight.

When I woke up again, I was shocked to find it was already 9 a.m. and Mike had obviously left the house for work in ninja mode. I couldn't recall the last time I had slept in so late. I knew Daniel would be asleep still, but with a schedule to attend to, I was committed to waking him at 10. Before that, however, I had important calls to make, so I pulled on my dressing gown – I could shower and dress later – and headed down to put the kettle on.

'Oh God, Casey,' Christine said, after I'd told her what had been happening in the week since Daniel came to us. 'I'm so sorry to hear that. Are you and Mike okay?'

'We're okay,' I said, opting not to use my usual, breezy 'fine!' 'At the moment, that is, but this is all very draining. Disturbed sleep, defiant teenager and no respite from it at all. We need this education thing sorting fast, as in straight away, and I'm afraid it's a deal-breaker, Chris – we're getting too old for this!'

'I agree,' she said immediately. 'Not about you guys being too old,' she added hurriedly. 'Not at all – you're like bloody Peter Pan, Casey. Put the rest of us to shame. But yes, about the education. They should have been organising that the minute he came out of the children's home.'

But had they been? Somehow I doubted it. 'I don't bloody feel like Peter Pan,' I said. 'And how fast do you think we can get that sorted?'

'Faster than a speeding bullet,' she said firmly. 'Just you watch me.'

True to her word – well, almost – Christine called me back just over an hour later, just as I was making up a tray of food for Daniel, who, perhaps predictably, had proved almost impossible to rouse at the first attempt. And, cross as I was with him – because I *had* put my trust in him – I was in no mood for fighting or cajoling either.

'Okay,' she said, without preamble. 'Assuming you're free, Phoebe and I will come out to see you this afternoon – and Daniel, of course – to discuss an education package we are currently scraping together.'

'You've managed to get him something?' Despite my bullish tone earlier, I was genuinely shocked by how quickly this had happened.

'In theory, yes – just a few details still need to be thrashed out. But I'm confident we'll have it all in place by the time we get to you.'

Christine's news changed my mood completely. I'd been lying in bed chuntering about all the bureaucracy I'd probably have to wade through and it had all been put in place with one phone call! It made me feel so much more positive that after showering and dressing, I flung open all the downstairs windows and embarked on a mopping and vacuuming spree with my golden oldies radio station blasting away at full volume – something I'd not normally do with a sleeping child above me. Tough, I thought. Sleep disturbance works both ways.

But Daniel slept so deeply, it had zero effect and neither did my usual ritual of food stuffs and half-hourly promptings. In fact, by the time Phoebe and Christine arrived, he was only just up and dressed, with half another sunny September day already gone.

This was another worry in itself. Daniel had barely left the house in a week, repelling all suggestions of walks and shopping and so on. I had no idea what relationships he was still maintaining since coming to us, but at no point had he so much as mentioned any kind of social life, let alone taken himself off out. I knew being extricated from the gangs he was apparently hanging around with was part of the reason for moving him into foster care, but was that it now? Did he have no friends apart from Bella? Not that he'd ever mentioned her. And if that *was* true, how was he to make any? Well, apart from the ones he joshed and argued with in the virtual world, of course. Because, in common with a worrying minority, of young boys especially, that was clearly where he mostly lived. Apart from a couple of short mooches round the back garden with Mike – keen to show off his 'lockdown workshop' and try to enthuse the lad about something – he'd barely seen daylight. He'd soon be short on vitamin D, if he wasn't already.

Like me, however, both Phoebe and Christine were making the most of the Indian summer, the pair of them dressed as if for an impromptu garden party, in long floral dresses and, in Phoebe's case, accessorised with fuchsia-coloured loafers that matched her pink glasses precisely.

I showed them in, hoping their cheerful attire would be matched by cheering news, and could see right away that Phoebe was looking pleased with herself as she took her proffered seat. It was good to see. Because if she had pulled this off, then everything would now change.

'So,' she said, 'you'll be happy to know we've managed to secure a place for Deejay from next Monday at a facility called the Vines Centre, which is attached to a big comprehensive school.' She then named it and I knew it, back from the days when I worked in a school myself. As far as I could recall, it was some distance away from where we lived, but it could have been on the moon, frankly, and I'd still have been happy.

'That's great news!' I enthused.

'Just two afternoon sessions for now,' she hurried on, 'but at least it's a start.'

I looked from her to Christine, open-mouthed now. Because this bit wasn't so great. 'Only *two*?'

'For now, yes. That's all they can offer, sorry.'

'And only afternoons? Could it not be all day? Because that's kind of defeating the object, to be honest. The biggest obstacle we're facing in making progress with Dan is that he's been living a mostly nocturnal – and online – life for so long. I was hoping to get him into a morning routine, so that we can break his current sleeping pattern. Why can't he go for two full days and then build up to more?'

Christine looked embarrassed. 'It was the only facility that we knew would willingly take him, to be honest with you,' she said. 'Within our region anyway. What with his expulsions and behaviours … Well, as you can imagine, they were reluctant – we had to practically strong-arm them into it.'

'Indeed, we did,' Phoebe added. 'And it's only afternoons because they just have so many kids currently – they have to break the sessions down into blocks, so some will only have mornings. The good thing is, they did promise that a couple of kids are due to finish their final exams very soon and, if appropriate, and possible, they will consider giving some extra slots to Deejay when those kids leave. So that's promising, isn't it?'

Breaking Point

She looked at me with a smile so big and self-satisfied that my principal feeling was how much I'd have liked to wipe it off her face – metaphorically, at least, for a couple of reasons. One, for what I considered to be a half-hearted attempt to help this boy back onto the right tracks, and two, for still calling him Deejay. She wasn't his bro, or his bruh, she was his social worker. Just as we called our children by the names we had given them – and not the nicknames their friends did – some things were just the correct way to go about things. Silly, I know, both thoughts, but my frustration, and the inevitable weariness that comes with broken nights, were by now getting the better of me. I made an effort to compose myself and returned the smile.

'Well,' I said, trying hard to hang onto my positive mindset, 'I suppose it's better than nothing. And at least it's likely to meet with approval from upstairs. I'll go get *Dan* down, shall I?' I suggested. 'See how he reacts. I had hoped that he'd be receptive, but after last night's shenanigans, I'm no longer sure.' I stood up. 'Assuming he's not gone back to sleep again, that is.'

I noticed Christine trying to supress a smile as she clearly caught my emphasis on his name.

'Tell you what, Phoebe, why don't you go up and tell Dan about the package yourself?' she suggested. 'I know you'll have to physically see him in situ anyway today, as part of the moving-in deal, so you might as well reconnect up there and test the waters, hey? Just the two of you.'

'Two bloody afternoons a week?' I whispered to Christine as soon as Phoebe had headed off upstairs. 'Is that really the best they can do?'

Christine nodded. 'Sad to say, it is, at least right now. And I have to tell you, the sessions are only two hours long. As Phoebe said, demand is so high, they've had to break the school day up into blocks to be able to offer something to more kids, but at least it's quite a distance away. I checked on the way here and it's a 45-minute drive, so in all he'll be gone for around four hours, give or take, which is something, isn't it? At least a little respite for you a couple of times a week.'

'But what about all the other days?' I began. 'He literally *lives* in that bedroom. Yes, he's been coming down for his evening meal – Mike's insisted on that, though it often feels like we're pulling teeth, trying to get him to talk to us – but a lad his age shouldn't be holed up indoors, day after day. He needs activity, exercise. A chance to—'

I was stopped in my tracks by the sound of a commotion upstairs. We both stood up and, naturally, rushed out into the hall, the better to hear what was going on. And as we started up the stairs, it was all too obvious: another row.

'I said fuck off out my room!' Daniel yelled. 'I don't give a fuck what you have to say!'

'Well, that may be so,' Phoebe replied crisply, 'but you'll hear me out anyway. Because you need to know, DJ, that we have put some schooling in place for you at a place called the Vines Centre, in the afternoons, twice a week. So, starting from next Monday, and, from then on, every Monday and Thursday, a taxi will be coming here at noon to take you to there and then again, after school, to—'

The next thing we heard a yelp and a bang, followed by the slamming of Daniel's bedroom door. But, as Phoebe appeared at the top of the stairs and began scuttling back down them, we could still hear Daniel's voice, loud and clear. 'I said fuck OFF, you stupid bitch!' he roared. 'Leave me ALONE!'

Phoebe's cheeks, I noticed, were now as pink as her glasses. 'Well,' she said, rubbing the side of her head, 'that went well.'

'What on earth just happened?' Christine asked.

'Well, if you'll pardon my French, the little shit just threw a can of deodorant at me! *Jeez*,' she added, as she reached us, 'I am getting too old for all this.'

Tell me about it, I thought miserably.

Chapter 7

The days following the meeting with Christine and Phoebe were quite calm but it didn't take a genius to work out why: he'd had a stay of execution. As long as he agreed to come out with one or other of us at some point every day, even if it was just for a walk around the block, Daniel could have a whole week of late Wi-Fi – well, so long as he didn't nullify it by waking us up during the night. And though I was dismayed at the wait – I'd have liked to get him into school that same week, ideally – I decided it would benefit everyone if we spent the run-up without having any major confrontations and if we fostered a harmonious atmosphere at home, he'd be more likely to play ball once school began.

Not that the place that was taking Daniel was school in the sense that most people understood the term. The Vines Centre was a facility that took in teenage boys and girls who had been excluded from mainstream education during their final one or two years at school and who still needed to acquire at least a couple of exam results before the official leaving age. The structure of each day, apparently, was less important than the time it took to get a child through enough learning in order to gain some form of qualification and that was why short bursts of intensive learning, in very small groups, seemed to be the theme there. Hence our two hours, twice-weekly, being seen as adequate – at least for now.

But at least we had something concrete to work towards and I decided I would start with some clothes shopping. This new school didn't actually have a uniform policy, but having seen most of Daniel's clothes, I knew I'd have to buy him a couple of suitable outfits, plus a hoodie or two, to see him through the term. This news pleased him no end and within minutes of me suggesting we might go out shopping together, my phone started pinging like crazy with screen shots and links to the most expensive tracksuits, trainers and hoodies I'd ever seen in my life. I knew I had an allowance for his clothing – as, no doubt, did he – but the list ran to several hundred pounds.

'I'm sorry, Dan,' I said, as I went back upstairs into his room, 'but there's no way on this earth I can afford to buy you stuff at those prices and we don't have those shops in town. Why don't you get dressed and we can have a walk round and see if we can get similar things, but cheaper?'

'I don't do cheap,' Dan said, looking at me as if I were mad. 'Everyone I know wears designer gear. They'll take the piss if I go into a new school looking like a tramp in cheap shit. Anyway, why d'we have to go to town? You not heard of' – he added finger quotes – 'like, "online"?'

I was tempted to point out that of course I had, but that I would very much like to get him, and me, out of the house. But there seemed little point in rising to it. 'Well,' I said instead, 'it looks like we have a problem then, don't we?' Because those prices are definitely not within my budget.' I lifted my phone. 'The trainers you sent me the link for – they're almost £200 on their own. You have to realise, most people just don't have that kind of money, myself included, especially when we need to get you all the other stuff as well. Come on, get yourself dressed and let's go look. Quite apart from anything else, you still need to get out of the house today, anyway, and why not make it something you'll enjoy doing?'

Daniel reluctantly admitted that he could do without new trainers until his birthday, which was in November, but still insisted that he wouldn't wear 'shitty' tracksuits and then, in a curveball I hadn't seen coming, begged me to make an online order as he said he 'suffered from social anxiety' and couldn't possibly go into town.

'I'll go down the park with you, but I swear down, I can't face doing town.'

Breaking Point

'This is news to me, Dan,' I said. 'Since when? Because I'm pretty sure there's nothing in your file about that.'

'There wouldn't be,' he replied immediately. 'I've not said nothing about it to anyone. It just, like, came on a few months back. You know, panic attacks and stuff – when I'm, like, in town and that, round loads of people.'

I studied his face carefully. Was this for real or was I right to feel suspicious? After all, he'd not mentioned it once in relation to him going to school. And if it *was* real, why hadn't he said so? Feigned or truthful, it would have given him a greater justification for school avoidance than he'd so far offered – at the very least it would have prompted social services to intervene with some kind of counselling or CBT. But perhaps that was the last thing he wanted. But *was* it for real? Oh, I wished I could work this lad out.

'Look,' he said, holding his phone up, 'there's no need anyway. This is a great online discount sports shop. I'll send you the link, shall I? Bet we can find everything there. Bet there'll be branded stuff on there – you know, last season stuff – that's okay with your budget, if you don't have enough, like, for the stuff that's out right now.'

I decided there was little point in arguing about us going out to the shops together. I'd park this new development for further thought later. In the meantime, having agreed, I went back downstairs and my phone was soon pinging with links to specific items that he obviously deemed acceptable. And he was right; the suggestions he'd made were all within my budget, so I ordered two sets of tracksuit bottoms, five T-shirts and three hoodies. It was still a small fortune, and far more than I'd ever spend on clothes for myself or Mike, but I figured that an investment in the boy now might encourage him to feel that we were in his corner, which in turn might help to give him confidence in taking his next step. I texted him the order confirmation with photos of everything and thankfully, he seemed happy about it, so even though I hadn't got him out of the house in the way I'd really wanted, it still felt like a success.

All in all, I had almost a full week of relative peace and quiet – and, crucially, free of the conflict that we'd 'enjoyed' the previous fortnight. That didn't, however, equate to a full week of restful nights, because, to my surprise, it seemed my brain had adjusted to being alert through the small hours, just waiting for a crash, bang or shout. Not Mike, though; he slept like a baby. Which I was pleased about, obviously, as he worked long, physical days managing a busy warehouse. I just wished that I could do the same. When I thought about it, I reasoned that it was my brain's way of protecting me from potential danger, but all I wanted was to tell it I was fine and let me bloody sleep! Get some shut-eye in the bank because I knew the biggest hurdle was now upon us – would he get up and go to school, as promised, or would we be back in our domestic war zone?

On the Sunday night, as had been agreed – and reminded of regularly to Daniel – the Wi-Fi would be turned off at 11 p.m., so we could be reasonably hopeful of him getting up okay on Monday morning. But at 10 p.m., while Mike and I were sitting on the sofa with a coffee, ready to catch up on the news, Daniel came into the living room.

Here we go, I thought, lowering my coffee mug.

Daniel gave us an apologetic half-smile. 'Sorry to disturb you guys,' he said, 'but please, is there any way you can leave the Wi-Fi on till midnight after all? I know it's supposed to be 11 tonight but the taxi doesn't come for me till 12, so it's not like I have to be up super early. *Please*, I beg. Just for tonight. I know the deal, and I'm not taking the piss, honest – it's just that I'm involved in something with some guys and I can't just leave halfway through.'

So, how did we respond? I glanced at Mike, my first instinct being to let it go – he'd asked very nicely, after all. And, to be fair, with the taxi not due until noon, he'd still get sufficient sleep. Mike caught my look – which had now gone from questioning to hopeful – then he shook his head slightly and looked at Daniel with a stern expression.

'Okay, fine,' he said. 'Just for tonight, if it matters so much. But I *mean* it, Dan,' he went on, cutting Daniel's whoop of delight off in its tracks, 'there'd best be no nonsense in the morning, you hear me? No giving Casey any of your back chat. And no arguments tonight when it goes off, either.'

Daniel was almost hopping from foot to foot in his eagerness to get back to his online bros. 'I swear there won't be, Mike. Promise. And I'll be up tomorrow, swear down, and, really, *really*, thanks.' He then left and bounded full speed back to his room.

'Don't say a word, Casey,' Mike said, before I could thank him myself. 'I swear you're making me into a soft touch, like you are.'

'I wasn't going to,' I said, grinning.

'Yeah, right,' said Mike. Then, as he picked up his coffee, 'How about you fetch me a chocolate biscuit to go with this? I think I deserve it, for my forbearance, don't you? Just the one, mind – I'll get back on track tomorrow.'

I smiled. He was right, he did deserve it. He'd barely touched a snack since his weight gain had been noted. Plus, he genuinely wanted to keep in good shape as, once he had the knee op, he'd be hobbling around for a while, unable to exercise. So, I leapt up and went to pay a visit to my designated snack cupboard, something I'd had, pretty much, since my own kids had been small and which now, for my grandchildren, was the stuff of legend. They all knew where it was, and the delights it always held – various types of crisps and crackers, all the chocolate bars they favoured, biscuits of all kinds and small, individually wrapped cakes.

Breaking Point

It wasn't a free-for-all, however. The kids knew to always ask if they wanted to take a snack after having a meal, or for supper if they were staying over, and I was always happy to explain our 'snack etiquette' to any other children who might be staying with us. But now, as I opened the door, in search of our chocolate digestives, I was shocked to find the cupboard half-empty. When I knelt down to have a proper look inside, I couldn't believe my eyes. It was stuffed with empty wrappers; even some that had been torn open but not actually eaten – just a bite taken from the cake it had contained. Plus, there was not a single bag of crisps to be found and I had definitely bought two different multi-packs on my last big shop. As for the biscuits, there were only slim pickings and no sign of the almost-full packet of chocolate digestives that had been there a few days back – i.e. the last time Mike had wanted anything from there.

So, it had to be Daniel. No question. I knew none of my kids or grandkids would ever do such a thing and, besides, with them all busy with school and friends, and our hands currently full, none of them had had set foot in the house since he'd come to us.

I rummaged around, gathering wrappers as I went, and eventually found a two-finger Kit-Kat. And I decided, then and there, that this was something that could wait. Daniel had obviously been coming downstairs in the small hours, in search of food, and had simply helped himself. Which I supposed was fair enough – he'd been hungry (and then some). But not to say anything to me about it, that needed addressing. Did he just assume I'd restock and no need to mention anything? I realised I had no idea how such things were dealt with at the children's home, so perhaps I should give him the benefit of the doubt. They might have a stock of snacks with a help yourself policy, after all. Still, it unsettled me, knowing he'd been prowling around the house looking in all our cupboards while we slept. What else might he think he was free to help himself to? Might he decide to crack open one of Mike's beers? I had the strongest sense yet, though I knew full well he was a child still, that we had an almost fully-grown man under our roof, about whom I still felt I knew so little.

But that was for tomorrow. And *after* school, which was when I decided would be the best time to sit down with him for a chat. In the meantime, it seemed sensible not to mention it to Mike either and, happily, he didn't query that I hadn't brought his favourite digestive – he simply opened the Kit-Kat I handed him and devoured it in seconds.

The next morning, I woke up with a mixture of emotions. I was happy that it was a nice, sunny day and that we had finally managed to get Daniel into a school, albeit for only two short periods per week, but I also felt nervous and a little bit sick. *Please let this be easy*, I asked the universe as I got into the shower, but it seemed the universe wasn't listening.

Breaking Point

'Come on, Dan, please!' I said as I placed some chocolate toast and a glass of milk on his bedside cabinet. It's 11.15, the taxi will be here in 45 minutes and this is the second time I've had to come up. Get up, get dressed and have your breakfast.'

Daniel growled loudly and once again pulled the duvet over his head and turned his back on me. I was so tempted to drag the bloody thing off him, but instead I opened the curtains and his bedroom window.

'I mean it, Dan, get up,' I said. 'Your new clothes are all there for you to put on and the deal was that you'd get up with no arguments and get ready to go in the taxi. Now *move* it, come *on*.'

'Leave me the fuck alone!' he barked from beneath the covers. 'I'm tired! I need 10 more *minutes*!'

'You can stop using that language right now!' I said, my anger rising like a tide. 'I'll be back up at 11.30 and you best be out of that bed, kid, I mean it.'

But, of course, he wasn't. I went up to his bedroom at five-minute intervals, the last attempt being at noon itself, and with the taxi already parked outside.

Which I duly pointed out – it could be clearly seen from his window.

'I don't *care*!' he yelled. 'I ain't going to no fucking *school*!'

I felt all my anger turn to impotent frustration because there was absolutely nothing I could do about it. And why on earth had I dared to hope that he *would* go? 'I tell you what, Dan,' I said finally, 'I can't physically drag you out, so it's your choice. But I can promise you this, there is no way in hell that you will be playing anything online – being online *full stop* – until you have been to school. Do you understand?'

'So, fucking what!' he yelled. 'And you really think you're that clever? My social worker topped my phone up, so I've been gaming using my hot spot, you fucking muppet!'

I was stunned into silence while my brain tried to make sense of what he'd just said to me. Without replying, I turned around and walked out of his bedroom, down into the hall and then out onto the street, where I informed the taxi driver that he'd be giving Daniel no lift today.

'I'm so sorry you've had a wasted journey,' I finished.

'No worries, love,' the driver said. 'I get paid either way so I'll see you this time Thursday and we'll try again.'

As he drove off, I wondered how familiar an occurrence this was. From his breezy tone, I reckoned it happened relatively often and for some reason, the thought of there being other Caseys, in other towns and cities, all battling through the same frustrating process as I was right now, gave me comfort, made me feel less alone. It also reminded me to keep tempering my expectations because I didn't have a magic wand. Expecting teenagers to comply with things they had already agreed wasn't just about telling them to in the moment; it was the result of long years of toiling at the parenting coalface. As the taxi driver had suggested, all I could do was try again.

I went back inside and rang the Vines Centre to speak to my contact there: the centre secretary, a Mrs Mathers.

'Not to worry,' she said, once I'd explained what had happened. 'Might be a case of first-day jitters, but please do try again on Thursday, because now he's on roll, it really is your responsibility to get him here. Don't you have transport of your own?'

Once again, I was stunned. Both at the suggestion and because of the image it conjured – of me trying to wrestle Daniel down into my car. 'Well, yes, I do,' I said, 'but Dan's entitled to transport and also, if he won't get up for the taxi, he won't get up for me either. He's six foot tall and built like a body builder, how am I supposed to do that?'

'Even so,' Mrs Mathers continued, 'the onus is on you to get him to us, Mrs Watson. We simply provide the education.'

'I'm not asking you personally to come get him,' I snapped. 'I'm simply informing you that today it won't be happening. But, yes, of course I'll try again on Thursday. Anyway, I have to go now,' I finished, my voice beginning to crack. 'I have other people to inform.'

The tears couldn't help but come. Tears of hopeless frustration. Because I could see it so clearly now: the same thing was going to happen on Thursday. And then next Monday, and next Thursday – because why should it be any different? What exactly did I think I was going to be able to change?

It suddenly felt like the whole world was against me and I didn't have the first clue what to do about it, especially now I'd learned about bloody Phoebe. What had the social worker been thinking? In topping up Dan's phone, and not bothering to let us know about it, she had made a mockery out of what we were aiming for; taken away the only sanction, realistically, that we had in our armoury. What were we supposed to do next? Refuse to feed him? Which was exactly the question, albeit rhetorical, that I posed to Christine, who, once I'd got over my snivelling, I phoned next.

'Oh, you poor thing,' she said. 'What a nightmare! But at least I can promise you that there will be no more phone top-ups from Phoebe. I'll get on to that immediately. The thing is, these days, kids of that age, we do have to give them access to a phone to make calls, as you know, but not a smartphone with internet access. Dan has no given right to having that. So, look, if it means we have to buy him a cheap pay-as-you-go, dial-and-call-only set-up from a supermarket, then that's what we'll do. And, in the meantime, how else can I help you? You know you only have to ask.'

'If you have someone who's able to come drag him out of bed, and dress him and physically carry him out to a taxi, that would be nice,' I suggested. 'Just Mondays and Thursdays, for now.'

Breaking Point

Christine laughed ironically. 'Oh, if only we could, eh? That would put the wind up him, for sure. But, listen. What I can do is find someone to come out and sit in for you, if that'll help. Give you a chance to get out for a few hours. I can literally sort that out for you right now ...'

'I'll be fine,' I insisted. 'I'm just offloading, it's been such a frustrating morning. No, honestly, it's okay. I probably will go out – he's old enough to be left alone in the house and I'm certainly not worried about him running off – quite the opposite. And if I do go out, the only thing at risk is my snack cupboard. So, you know, I'm thankful for small mercies and all that.'

Just chatting to Christine made me feel a whole lot better, but I was still too annoyed with Daniel to think about broaching the snack cupboard situation right now. And I wasn't going to tackle him about the Wi-Fi issue either. Given the situation with his phone top-up, that argument had already been rendered pointless. But since I knew Christine would now cut off that alternative supply of data, that was fine too. He would eventually run out of data, and probably quite soon. And then the real fun and games would begin.

Or, rather, they wouldn't, I thought, even managing to smile at my own pun. There was even a kind of poetry in it, I decided, as I went to make myself some lunch. All the power now lay in ... well, the power.

Chapter 8

Despite my resolve, and the knowledge that Daniel's 'hot spot' would soon be no more, I was on pins for the next two days, my thoughts all over the place. Aware as I was that I had probably been ridiculously optimistic, I was still angry with him for fooling us into believing he would honour our deal. I also hated that I'd almost lost my own temper in front of him and I still needed to confront him about the after-midnight snacking, which was continuing – something I had now discussed with Mike.

And I wished I'd done it sooner, because it really helped open the floodgates. As was so often the case when I got het up about things, Mike was able to break them down into their component parts – one of which, he pointed out, was *me*.

'Case,' he said as we sat together after tea on the Tuesday, 'you know what I don't get? You've never been this riled by a kid we've had before. What is it about this one that's upsetting you so much?'

Breaking Point

He then reeled off a list of some of the children we'd looked after, starting with Justin, our first, who'd not only stolen food, but smashed stuff up, and even kicked – pretty violently – our beloved family dog. 'And what about Jenson?' he added. 'Remember how hard he was to deal with? Or Sophia? And Spencer? Remember how challenged we were with them? What's different about Daniel that he's making you so stressed?'

'I don't know, love,' I said. 'I just can't seem to form a bond with him. I don't know if it's my age, or his age, or the fact that he towers over me, or what. I've no reason to believe he'd use physical force or anything, it's just that I dread confronting him about anything and that's so bad for a foster carer, isn't it?'

'No, it's not, Case,' Mike said firmly, taking my hand and squeezing it. 'Especially these days. And don't forget why he's with us – because no one else would have him and for precisely those reasons, I imagine.' He sighed. 'And, the bottom line is that everything's changing. Bloody kids are led to believe they can basically do what they like, when they like and entirely without consequence, in most cases. They watch all kinds of crap on their bloody smartphones and if you ask me, that's where a lot of the problems lie, so you're right to be weary and on guard, love. It's sad, but it's a fact of modern life.'

'But we can't live like this, Mike,' I said. 'It's horrible! I never thought I'd get to a stage in my career where I feel the way I do now, where I wake up every day feeling anxious. There's a part of me that actively wants Daniel to stay up there, sleeping, because it's the only time I get a bit of peace.'

'Love, the only way you're going to get that, in this situation,' Mike said, 'is if you completely go against your usual instincts.' Then he smiled. 'I know it'll sound funny to you, but when the lad makes you feel like that, before you react, stop and ask yourself, what would Mike do?'

I couldn't help but laugh, just imagining myself doing that, eyes up to the heavens, asking Jesus for guidance. But it was a perceptive thing to say, because, despite our having each other's backs all the time, Mike and I had very different ways of dealing with children. We always had, and yet, somehow, the combination worked: with me being instinctively very trusting and loving, and quick to find excuses to explain behaviours, where Mike was pragmatic, always able to see the big picture – and always at a safe enough emotional distance not to be blinded by illusions. And his solution – what would Mike do? – seemed sound. To forget that I lost my temper, because all adults do sometimes – it's also healthy and helps clear the air. And so what about the snacks? They're just bloody snacks – and the kid must have been hungry!

'Tell him you've noticed,' he counselled. 'And from now on, take him snacks up at bedtime, but with the proviso that once they're gone, they're gone. And as for feeling angry with him for reneging on your "deal" …

well, you'll just have to swallow that. But, Case, you know – when you make promises about consequences, you *have* to follow them through. No tweaks, and absolutely no backing down. You've already given more than enough ground in that department – and I hold up my hands here for letting you. And he's proven several times now that he doesn't respect that, so, while I understand the reasons – he's had a seriously messed up "childhood", and I sympathise, I really do – if we keep hoping for the best from him, we're delusional and that's definitely not helping. Honestly, love,' he finished, 'we have to fight fire with fire now – you'll feel so much better if you just accept things for how they really are. How *Daniel* really is, instead of just hoping for this miracle new child to suddenly emerge from that toughened shell. In a nutshell, don't try so hard to change the things you can't – just change the way they make you feel.'

I stared at my husband, knowing he was right and wishing like mad that I had his capacity to remain so calm and unaffected by things. Also, how did he get so much bloody wiser than me all of a sudden?

'I'll try,' I said. 'Because you're spot on, I know you are, and that kid's up there, happy as Larry, unaware that I'm down here cracking up over him. Things have to change and you're right – that starts with me, I guess.'

'Aware or unaware, it doesn't matter,' Mike said. 'What matters is how we react. You need to get back to being you. Go out and do the shopping – he's old enough to be left if he doesn't want to go. Get yourself round to see the kids, or your mum and dad, play your music. Enjoy your days. Thing is, Case, the lad has to find a way to fit into *our* lives. We do all we can to make that possible, but if he's not taking it, that's his lookout. He will, eventually, but until then, stop putting your own life on hold.'

So, I stuck to my guns. There had been no internet on whatsoever for the rest of Monday and we did the same on Tuesday, secure in the knowledge that, despite his grand announcement, Daniel would have run out of the modest amount of data he'd had in no time. We still had it on our own phones of course, so we could still get online, but we could only watch 'old-school' TV. In the big scheme of things, of course, this mattered to us very little. Not at all, in fact, if we could just make it work.

Then, after conversations with both Phoebe and Christine, to run our plan by them both, we switched from the stick to the carrot approach. At teatime on Wednesday, therefore, we told Daniel that he would be allowed some time online so he could do a bit of gaming that evening, but ONLY because we expected he'd return the favour by getting up for school the next day. Despite his boast about the hot spot, this had obviously gone cold because he seemed happy to agree to anything.

But when we switched the Wi-Fi off at 10 p.m., as we'd already warned, everything immediately started kicking off upstairs.

Breaking Point

'What's going on?' Daniel shouted as he burst into the living room. 'It's nowhere near time for it to go off! Is it glitching? Only I'm halfway through a big game!'

'It's 10 o'clock, Dan,' Mike told him levelly.

'What the fuck?! No, it isn't!'

'I think we all know how to tell the time, lad,' Mike answered smoothly.

'But that's way too early!' he protested.

Mike now stood up. 'No, it's the time we agreed. You couldn't get up for school on Monday when the Wi-Fi went off at midnight, which is why we agreed 10 p.m. It's not up for debate, so please go back up to bed and get some sleep. And if you don't get up tomorrow, then you've broken the contract, so, again, there will be no internet whatsoever. The choice is yours, Dan. Ours has already been made – that's what's going to happen going forward.'

Daniel laughed, actually laughed in Mike's face. 'Yeah right, like you'd carry on going without your Sky telly and your own internet, just to piss me off.'

Mike laughed right back. 'It doesn't bother us, mate, not a bit. We barely watch Sky in any case – we only have it for the kids – and we can already access the internet on our phones. Anyway, like I said, it's your choice: you either go to school or you don't go. But you know the consequences: no school, no more Wi-Fi. And, by the way, there's no point in you thinking it won't matter because your social worker will top up your phone, because that won't be happening either. No going to school will also mean no more top-ups. If you need to make calls, you'll have to use one of our phones, but only if it's important. Either that or they said they'll buy you a pay-as-you-go, bog-standard supermarket phone. A burner phone, I believe they're called.'

There was a moment when I really thought Daniel was going to physically lash out, so furious was his expression and so tense were the muscles in his arms and his face. But Mike's physical presence was clearly enough to give him pause and after several long seconds, his body language changed – so much so that he almost seemed to shrink before our eyes. He then lowered his head, spun around and left the room without speaking, before thundering back off up the stairs. He did slam his bedroom door, which was only to be expected, but after that, there wasn't another peep from him.

'And tomorrow morning, Casey,' Mike said after we'd waited 10 minutes for a commotion that never came, 'do *not* stress yourself out like you did on Monday. Go wake him at 11 a.m., shout up half an hour later – do *not* keep going up and down those stairs – then call up finally, when the taxi comes and that's *it*. He knows the score now, so leave him to decide what he's going to do. No more of your "mountain to Mohammed" stuff, okay?'

Which was, of course, all so much easier said than done, especially for someone like me, and although I agreed with the strategy, I wasted no time in saying so. To which Mike replied, with an eye roll, that I should just listen to myself. Since when had I become someone who couldn't administer tough love, set boundaries and enforce them, take charge? Which could have made for a sleepless night, but in fact it proved the opposite. I drifted off with the words of the Vines Centre secretary, Mrs Mathers, in my ears: *It was my responsibility to get Daniel to school.* Bigger picture time, however; in reality, it wasn't. It was my responsibility to do what I could to facilitate *Daniel* taking that responsibility *himself*. Provide the wake-up call, take up the breakfast and let him know when the taxi arrived – there was literally nothing more I could do.

Having already figured out which snacks he liked best, from his small hours' forays, the following morning, I set a breakfast tray with cereal bars, a banana and a glass of milk, and took it upstairs to Daniel at 11. I then knocked on his bedroom door and when there was no response, steeled myself bodily, because no response was exactly what I'd expected. Only today, there would be no confrontation. I would stay just long enough to confirm that I'd woken him up and if he went back to sleep again, so be it.

I then opened the door and my mouth immediately fell open too. Not only was Daniel already awake, he was also up, fully dressed and sitting at his desk – he even had his coat on!

Determined not to make a big deal of this astounding state of affairs, I placed the breakfast things beside him on the desk.

'There you go, kiddo,' I said brightly. 'If you don't fancy eating now, just drink the milk and take the other bits with you. I'll shout up when the taxi arrives.'

'Thanks,' Daniel said, picking up the glass and even gracing me with a smile before I left.

I was in shock, and even more so when he rattled down the stairs only seconds after the taxi pulled up. He must have been watching for it from his window.

'See you later, then,' he said as he sauntered out the front door, cereal bars in hand. 'And cheers for these.' And then he was gone.

Wow, I thought, *maybe I should listen to Mike more often*. I waited at the door until the car was out of sight. Had that really just happened? There was still a part of me that couldn't quite believe it really had – or that, at any moment, he'd reappear, having bailed from the taxi. It had been such a long time since he'd been in any sort of educational establishment, after all. And although there'd been not another word about his 'social anxiety' – a ploy, surely? – he would still, I was sure, be pretty nervous. But as the first hour ticked by, with no return home and no phone call from the school, I could only assume things must have gone to plan. It was only a first step, of course, because things might be going badly, but I refused to start doomscrolling down negative thoughts. Only positives, positives, positives … In which frame of mind, I decided to call the children's home. I'd promised I'd keep June Hicken, the manager, updated on progress and even though this first day going to school was hardly progress, I had already decided that I ought to check back in with her anyway to ask a few more general questions about Daniel, and particularly if she had any ideas about how I might entice him out of the house with me somewhere further than the park at the end of our road.

'Oh, I'm afraid Mrs Hicken isn't in today,' the male voice that had answered the phone said. 'I'm Paul Cater, assistant manager. Can I help?'

I explained that I just wanted to let Mrs Hicken know that we'd managed to get Daniel into a school and to just update her on his progress.

'Oh, so you guys have young Dan, then,' the man said. 'How are things going? It was such a relief to get him placed in a family, so hats off to you. Is he settling in okay?'

'I wouldn't say that, exactly. I mean, it's really good news that we've managed to get him some schooling – only part-time as yet, and to be honest, it's only the first day so it could still all go pear-shaped – but I'd be lying if I said he was settling in well. It's been a tough few weeks. Actually, the "in" part *is* correct. Apart from local walks, which we've insisted on, he's not left the house. But when we do winkle him out, generally by trading fresh air for the promise not to switch off the Wi-Fi, it's torture. I keep up a constant stream of chatter, he grunts back in monosyllables and more often than not, walks three paces ahead of me anyway, as if he's the monarch and I'm a lady-in-waiting. He games constantly, of course – you probably already know that – but, honestly, he lives like a hermit.'

Paul chuckled. 'Now that's not a term I've ever heard used in relation to the lad! I mean, initially, yes. He was very intimidated by the older kids when he first came here – you probably already know that – but latterly, the problem was the exact opposite. He was always off somewhere, usually never to be found until he decided it was time to come back. Hence our being so anxious to get him away from here.'

Which, of course, I did know. And it sat so at odds with how he'd been since he'd come to us, so I said so.

But Paul Cater seemed to think he knew why. 'He had a really close friend here. An older lad called Joshua, a 17-year-old. Thick as thieves, those two. Always on the streets, getting into trouble, selling drugs for the older dealers and, more often than not, being brought back by the police. It was the situation with Joshua that made us apply pressure to get Daniel moved.'

He then explained that just before Daniel left the children's home, his friend Joshua had received a two-month custodial sentence in a Young Offender Institution (YOI). 'So that may well be the reason why Dan is currently lying low. Not because there's trouble coming his way, I hasten to add, but because he's probably waiting till he can hook up with him again, get hold of some money.'

'From where?' I asked, not really wanting to know the answer. Which came anyway.

Breaking Point

'From Joshua. Once he's out – which will probably be imminent; if he behaves himself he'll only do a month – odds are he'll be back on the streets dealing and will send some money to Dan, to get the team back together. I imagine that'll be what Dan's waiting on, anyway.'

It occurred to me at that moment that I hadn't actually given Daniel any of his £10-per-week pocket money yet. I'd set it aside for him, but as foster children were expected to save some of their allowance, and he hadn't yet asked for anything – not that he'd been anywhere to spend any – I'd simply been transferring it weekly into my own savings account, intending to give it to him if he asked for a new game download or something else. I knew from experience that these games could run to upwards of £50, so they were definitely items that we encouraged the kids to save up for. But then another thought occurred to me:

'But how will he get it to him? You think he'll come here?'

'Wouldn't need to,' Paul said. 'Dan has a bank account. He can just ping it there. Or, rather, *could*. Fingers crossed that's never going to happen. We had a meeting with Joshua's social worker last week and she's currently trying her level best to get him moved out of the area the minute he's released. For his own good, of course, but also for Dan's sake. If those two reconnect, it'll be a recipe for disaster; they'd both end up inside eventually.' He chortled again. 'You don't happen to have a clone in another county, by any chance, do you?'

Dark humour, obviously. But, like Mike, I could tell this was a man who'd seen plenty and while he obviously took his job very seriously, was able to display the same healthy detachment. But it was depressing news, even so. Much as it potentially answered the question about Daniel's apparent lack of interest in going out and socialising, if true, it was dispiriting to think he was just biding his time, waiting for his buddy to be released so he could pick up where he left off. I could only pray that this Joshua kid did get moved right away. Because if he didn't, something told me that getting Daniel going to school regularly would soon become the least of our problems.

Chapter 9

The first thing I had to deal with, and that I'd almost forgotten about, was my upcoming birthday, but, more importantly, the celebrations for my grandson Carter's fourth birthday. I had spoken to Riley already, and Kieron as well, and thankfully they had both agreed that I would simply share Carter's party, because I really didn't feel like making a fuss this year.

'But, Mum,' Kieron had pleaded, 'let's at least do something. You normally love parties, what's wrong with you?'

'It's not like it's a big one or anything,' I said, 'and honestly, when we get the chance, me and your dad are going to go off on a mini-break somewhere to commemorate our birthdays. I just think this time, and especially as Dan is living with us, two celebrations in the space of a week would be just a bit much.'

Not only did they concede, but all three of my kids, Riley, Kieron and Tyler, plus all of their partners, of course, agreed that I wouldn't have to lift a finger to help.

'It's your day too, Mum,' Riley said, 'so we're all chipping in with everything. I've booked the community centre, our Kieron's booked a face painter and bouncy castle, and Naomi and Ty are making all the food at mine, once they arrive. All we need you to do, if it's okay, is pay for the cake. I've sent you a link to the cake lady, oh, and the DJ, we decided to sort out a fun DJ. That sound okay?'

I laughed. So much for not lifting a finger – I'd certainly be lifting my purse, if nothing else!

Much as I pleaded with Daniel to come with us to the party, he really, really did not want to go.

'Please, Casey, I beg!' he said. 'I hate kids' parties, I swear down. I can't even understand what's so good about 'em. I never had parties and it didn't do me no harm, did it?'

Though I dutifully smiled at that, it made me feel sad. But I guess what you never had you don't miss.

'I suppose I could leave you here and just phone you now and again to check in,' I said, even though I was reluctant to do so, 'and maybe I could pre-order you a pizza or something to be delivered?'

'Yeah, cheers,' Daniel said, adding, 'double pepperoni with BBQ base. Please can you order me that?'

'I'll do you a deal,' I said. 'I'm happy to leave you home alone and order your pizza, if you agree that you'll at least come for a walk with me on the morning.

Breaking Point

A decent walk this time, not just a forced march up and down our road. I'll just show you around the neighbourhood a bit – where the park is, where the local shop is, nothing drastic.'

At first, Daniel looked horrified, but as I stood, hand on hips, eyebrows raised, he relented. 'Fine, I'll do that,' he said, 'but not too long, and definitely no shops or anything, and nowhere there'll be loads of kids or 'owt, 'cos that's just embarrassing.'

I rolled my eyes. 'Deal,' I said. 'Oh, and I'll try not to embarrass you,' I added as I left his room.

So that's exactly what we did. Daniel reluctantly got up early and accompanied me for a quick tour of the local area. As per usual, I couldn't get much out of him by way of chit-chat as he had his hood pulled tightly around his head and face, but it was definitely progress of a sort.

I also managed to really enjoy the first full day out I'd had since Daniel had come to us. And not because it was a momentous event, or anything. It was just lovely to catch up with everyone and feel normal. My sister Donna and her grandkids were there too, and it was lovely to spend time with them. Also, to see my mum and dad – though they obviously parked themselves at a table right at the back, away from all the kids running around. The little ones were shrieking noisily in delight as the DJ fashioned balloons into silly shapes and sculptures, and then chased around the room with them, like a four-year-old himself.

Little Carter absolutely loved his green birthday cake, with its lurid icing and Hulk hand bursting out of the centre, and he was thrilled with the Marvel scooter that Mike and I had bought him. I also got the opportunity to tell Riley all about Daniel and the worries I had about what might happen if his old friend did indeed re-appear on the scene. She listened and sympathised, of course, but as is so often the case with Riley, who is every inch her father's daughter, she didn't seem to see it as such a big deal.

'No point worrying about the might be's, Mum,' she said, 'and until you hear something to the contrary, just take a leaf out of Dad's book and chill.'

'I need the *whole* book to do that,' I answered wryly.

Though, having heard nothing, I was obviously worried about the situation with this Joshua character, my hunch being that perhaps Daniel hadn't heard anything either, because for the next fortnight, we seemed to be comfortably into some kind of routine and confrontations seemed to have become a thing of the past. There had been only one incident, on the second Monday, when he announced that he had a headache and so needed to skip school that afternoon, but I'd dealt with that by presenting him with two paracetamol and a glass of water, telling him that the medication would see him through the scant two hours he'd be there. And he hadn't even pushed back – just accepted them and took them – so perhaps he'd finally accepted our house rules. After all, Daniel wasn't stupid; he knew we – Mike especially – meant business and at least this way he was allowed the Wi-Fi at the weekends and on those days following the ones when he'd attended school.

I was still worried about the amount of time Daniel was spending in his room, however, but kept reminding myself of what Paul Cater at the children's home had told me; the alternative, at least for now, was likely to be far worse – only when Daniel was right away from the malign influences he'd been previously exposed to would some kind of healthy, age-appropriate social life begin to happen. And hopefully that *would* happen, once he was properly established in a school routine and, fingers crossed, attending more sessions. Even so, I didn't want to just leave him there festering all day when he wasn't in school, so I began insisting that, as well as getting out for a daily walk, he start joining me downstairs to eat his lunch.

He did try, to be fair, at least a few times. I would get him to pass me things, like the bread or something out of the fridge, and simply chatter away to him while he got them, so that at least I could get some form of conversation out of him, even if part of it was only grunts.

'You fancy bacon and mushrooms, or sausage and beans or your sandwich?' I asked, one time he came down for a drink just before lunchtime. 'In fact, while you're here, you might as well give me a hand.'

'Um, can I have bacon, but with beans?' he asked. 'I'm not keen on mushrooms. I don't mind 'em in, like, a curry or Bolognese and stuff, but not, like, in a sarnie – they go too slimy.'

Fair point. ''Course you can,' I said. Then, chancing my arm, 'What kind of stuff did your dad used to make when you lived at home?'

I took him off guard with that one, as I suspected I would, but after staring at me for a moment, Daniel just shrugged,

'I can't really remember,' he said, 'but mostly he'd give me money to go get shit from the shop, or the chippy. The kids' home was alright though, you know, for food an' that. They'd more or less let us have what we wanted, pretty much, and there was a good cook there – man, she made *really* nice puddings.'

Realising how quickly he'd moved the conversation on, I didn't push the probing any further. It was a long conversation to be having with Daniel and I didn't want to ruin it.

'Here's your sarnie,' I said, pushing a plate towards him, 'and you'll have to try and remember what those puddings were that you liked. I'm happy to have a go at them for you.'

I was also happy that we'd had our short conversation. It was the first time I had ever mentioned either of Daniel's parents and it could have gone really badly. Experience had taught me that with a kid like Daniel, baby steps were the way to go and in this brief interaction, I felt I'd achieved something, even if I wasn't sure what. I made a mental note to perhaps try again next

Breaking Point

time I caught him in such a good mood, and to let Christine know I'd made a little progress.

And so onwards we trundled. And the end of the second week, while Daniel was on his way home from school, his teacher called me to give me an update on progress. Which was unexpected, so my first thought was obviously, *Oh, no ... here we go ...*

But all was apparently well. 'Oh, it's nothing to worry about,' he was quick to reassure me. 'I'm Simon Kench, Daniel's teacher – just keeping you in the loop. We like to keep all interested parties informed. And, on the whole, he's getting on pretty well. Certainly better than his notes would have indicated.'

'On the whole?' I said, unable not to focus on potential negatives. 'Has there been an incident?'

'No, no – as I said, nothing for you to worry about. He doesn't manage a great deal of work, if I'm honest – can only manage about 10 minutes on a given task before he throws in the towel, so to speak, but that's to be expected. But at least it's a start – and it's something we can build on, week by week. It's been a long time since he's been in education, so we need to take things slowly. But he's generally receptive, and he certainly isn't causing us any problems, behaviour-wise.

'Oh, I see,' I said, relieved. 'And the other children in his group – is he getting along with them okay?'

'That's the thing,' he said cheerfully. 'It's a small class, and the friendship groups were already formed when Dan joined us, which I thought might create a problem with isolation. But it hasn't at all. They all seem to like him, and he them, and you'll be pleased to hear he's even made a friend now – a lad called Mikey, who actually attends the main comprehensive school.'

Mr Kench explained that the Vine Centre, which was situated in the grounds of a large comprehensive, was actually quite close to the school's main entrance. It was here that Daniel's taxi dropped him off for his session and they usually arrived early, which put him right in the middle of the main school's lunch break. He and Mikey would hang out together, apparently, until it was time to go in and, according to Mr Kench, had struck up quite a friendship. They both enjoyed gaming, or so Daniel had told him, and were now doing so online together, evenings and weekends.

Slightly irked as I was that Daniel seemed to be happier to chat to his teacher than either Mike or me, I couldn't help but feel pleased when I heard this news. It also rubber-stamped that I was right to press so hard for some schooling and would surely also help make the case for Daniel being granted some extra sessions.

'Wow!' I said. 'That's really good news, even if it would have been nice if the lad would be as forthcoming with us as he obviously is with you!'

Mr Kench chuckled. 'Teenage boys, eh?' he quipped.

'And re extra sessions,' I ventured, since there was no time like the present, 'I don't suppose there's any news on that yet?'

Breaking Point

Mr Kench chuckled again. 'Like gold dust, our sessions. But rest assured, as soon as a slot comes up for Dan, you'll be the first to know. But it's looking likely as one of the girls in our group is moving away to another area fairly imminently, so I might just have news on that in a fortnight or so. I'll check in weekly, in any case, so watch this space …'

I put the phone down, feeling a whole lot happier about everything. Maybe I didn't need to worry about Joshua after all. And although I knew nothing about the 'new kid on the block' I'd just been told about, the fact that Mikey was in the main school was a big plus and hopefully a new relationship to be encouraged. I'd have to see if Daniel would open up to me about him – perhaps that very afternoon.

As it turned out, though, I didn't even need to broach the subject. Daniel arrived home half an hour later and, full of smiles, he did so himself. Plus, he had a potentially welcome request: to be allowed to go and spend time with his new friend.

'Please, please, please, Casey, can I go for tea at my new mate's house tomorrow?' he asked, sounding – music to my ears – just like any other 15-year-old boy. 'His name's Mikey,' he added, 'and I swear, you'll really like him.'

Since it felt important that he should be left unaware that I'd been discussing this with his teacher, I made as if I knew nothing about this new friendship. 'Mikey? Is he one of the lads in your group?' I asked.

Daniel shook his head. 'Nah, he's in a regular class but the same year as me. He's safe, I swear down. And if I'm allowed to go, and you're okay with dropping me for the train and that, his mum says she's cool with dropping me back to the station near theirs so you can pick me up from this end. If that's okay with you, that is. About nine, kind of time. I can always walk if not,' he finished. 'It's no bother.'

'Of course we'll drop you off and collect you,' I assured him. 'But where do they live exactly?'

Daniel provided me with the name of the area where Mikey lived, which was some distance away – obviously the other side of the main school's catchment area.

'And you can have his mum's number to phone her,' he went on. 'Mikey gave it me. You know, so you can check her out an' that. Honest, it's all completely legit. And I'd really, really like to go.'

And I'd really, really like to 'check her out an' that', I decided. Due diligence. There was still the possibility that his plans were different, after all. 'Okay,' I said, 'let me have the number and I'll give her a ring in a bit. And I'll obviously have to run it by Phoebe as well.'

He frowned now. 'What's *she* got to do with it?'

'She is your social worker, love, so she has everything to do with it.'

He shrugged, seeming to think better of arguing with me. 'Okay, whatever. But make sure you tell her he's legit.'

Breaking Point

'Legit'? What did that even mean? I went into the snug to make my calls once Daniel had finished his tea and gone upstairs to play on his console. Mikey's mum was called Carol and, as promised, she knew all about the proposed visit and confirmed all the details Daniel had given me.

'Be nice to meet the lad,' she enthused. 'Mikey's been telling me all about him. And to be honest with you, I'm glad they seem to have hit it off so well because some of the lads my Mikey hangs around with – well, you know what lads are like – but this lot never seem to be able to keep from making mischief. In trouble with the police a couple of them, regularly. I mean, I know my lad can be a bit of a handful – can't they all? – but he's a good kid at heart. Just needs not to run with the wrong 'uns.'

I wasn't sure how to respond to all this unsolicited information, particularly since Mikey's mum clearly knew nothing whatsoever about the various mischiefs Daniel was very well documented as having been up to over the past couple of years. I supposed, just as Daniel had been at pains to do with me with Mikey, the lad himself had given him a glowing review. But Carol seemed frank, friendly and pretty no-nonsense – and I had a genuine affinity with any parent who was so obviously not blind to her child's shortcomings. In fact, I decided, it was refreshing. So, slight red flag though it was – two 15-year-old boys, both flagged as handfuls – when I ran it past Phoebe, it was from a position of largely seeing no problem in it myself, just as Daniel had hoped I would. He was going to a friend's house and his friend's mum would be there – there were definitely worse things he could be doing.

Phoebe agreed. 'Plus, it's good to see him establishing a bit of a social life, isn't it?' she said. 'Away from all those bad lads, back at the children's home. And it's only for a few hours after this Mikey finishes school tomorrow, so it's not like there's a lot of time to get into any mischief, is it? Let me know how things go.'

I duly dropped Daniel at the train station the following day at 2 p.m., revelling in the fact that, for the first time since he'd come to us, a month ago now, he was now heading off out to see an actual friend – a new friend he'd made in *real* life – on his own.

The station was only up the road from the school they attended, so the plan was that Daniel would meet Mikey outside the school gates and they'd walk together the 20 minutes it took to get to Mikey's house. Then, his mother having agreed to drop Daniel back at the station and wait with him till the train came, he would get on the 8.45 back to us.

I tried my hardest to keep myself busy in the sudden period of free time I'd acquired. I cooked a lovely steak dinner for me and Mike and then scrubbed the kitchen to within an inch of its life. Then I went upstairs and stripped Daniel's bed and washed and dried everything before making it up again. I cleaned and wiped round in his room and then finally, giving in to pressure from my husband, agreed to 'just sit down!' with Mike and watch some telly.

By 9 p.m., however, I had ants in my pants. I'd arranged for Carol to text me to let me know Daniel was safely on the train, but as yet I had heard nothing from her. Or Daniel, for that matter, though I'd texted him too – just to remind him which train he had to be on. I didn't want to seem overanxious, but as the minutes went by, it only seemed sensible to text Carol and ask her. So I did, and her text came back almost immediately: *yes, sorry!* she'd put. *Mikey says he definitely caught it.*

'What's this "Mikey says" bit?' I asked, showing Mike my phone screen.

'That he's on it,' he confirmed. 'What's the problem?'

'But I thought she was supposed to be taking him to the station.'

'Well, maybe she did and stayed in the car while his friend went to see him off at the platform. What of it? He's on the train, that's what matters. And I'm going to pick him up, in –' He consulted his watch. 'Twenty minutes.'

Which was plausible, but I just had a bad feeling about it. Which Mike could tell from my expression before I'd even voiced it.

'Or maybe she didn't,' he said. 'Maybe they walked to the station. Like I said, does it matter? He's 15, love.'

'But that wasn't the plan. He was going to Mikey's, then his mum was going to drop him, so—'

'So what?'

'So I texted him too and he didn't answer.'

'Perhaps he didn't have a signal. And stop pacing up and down,' he added, smiling. 'You'll wear the carpet out. We know he's on the train and I'll be off soon to pick him up. Why create problems we don't even know are problems?'

But some sixth sense had gripped me. Plus, it was Friday evening and there could be all sorts of drunks on that train. I hadn't thought it through and now my mind was imagining all kinds of things. 'I know. And I'm not creating problems,' I lied. 'I'm going to get my shoes on and come with you.'

Mike shook his head, obviously. 'If that's what you want to do …' he said, getting up from his armchair. 'But stop fretting. He's on the train and it's all going to be fine.'

But my gut feeling had been the right one – because it wasn't fine.

'He's staggering,' Mike observed when we finally picked Daniel out, from our vantage point in the near-empty car park. He was the last straggler from the dozen or so people who'd emerged from the station and looked distinctly unsteady on his feet as he scanned the parked cars, looking for ours. 'Bloody look at him!' Mike added, unbuckling his seat belt with a sigh. 'He looks drunk!'

'He does too!' I said, as Daniel acknowledged us with a flapping hand before weaving his way towards us, giggling at nothing.

Breaking Point

Mike got out and opened one of the car's back doors.

'Have you been drinking?' I asked as Daniel clambered awkwardly into the back seat, still giggling. I smelled the air then. 'Or have you taken something?'

'Nah, bruh,' he slurred, following it up with a belch. 'Wassup?'

Mike climbed back in, did his belt up and adjusted the rear-view mirror. 'Do you know how many kids and teenagers have been through our house, *bruh*? I'll tell you wassup, lad, you stink of bloody weed and don't bother saying you've been around people who had it but you haven't, because we've heard it all before. I can see you've been on it, and if that's what you think you're getting up to at this Mikey's, you can think again, mate.'

'*Okay*,' Daniel muttered, as he straightened himself up and started fumbling ineffectually for his own belt. 'Jesus, it was only one measly spliff! *And* I shared it,' he added, before either of us could answer. 'Chill *out*! It's no big deal, Mike. I mean, like, *everybody* does it.'

'No, they don't, lad,' Mike said, a tic pulsing in his jaw now.

Here we go, I thought miserably, as we pulled out of the station. We drove home in silence.

Chapter 10

The weekend turned out to be pretty quiet. Daniel just wanted to go straight to bed after his Friday night antics and although we had left the Wi-Fi connected, as per our deal, I was fairly sure that at no point did he use it.

I knew all about cannabis, of course. Because being drug-aware was considered to be part of our training, we had to attend courses annually to keep up with ongoing trends, which meant I also knew that modern cannabis was nothing like the weed smoked back in the sixties and seventies. It was particularly harmful, it was now known, to adolescent brains, so smoking it regularly at 15 was particularly dangerous. Trouble was that I knew what Daniel had said the previous night held a hefty dose of truth. Drugs *were* ubiquitous and every year, there seemed to be a worrying uptick in the number of teenagers who'd tried them. Plus, had it been *just* weed he'd taken? We didn't know. Although he seemed a little worse for wear as he took himself to bed,

Breaking Point

I made a point of checking on him half-hourly until we went to bed ourselves at midnight, where we lay awake for some time discussing this new development.

'So, that's what one spliff does for him, then?' I asked Mike as we lay in bed. 'I bet he'd had more than that.'

'You know, Casey, he might not have,' said Mike. 'Don't forget, according to his file, he's been a pretty heavy user over the years, despite his young age. He then comes to us, his best mate is in jail and, holed up in his room, far away from his "crew", he has zero access to anything. And how long's it been? Weeks now. If he's the habitual user he's supposed to be, I'd imagine he was getting pretty desperate to get hold of some weed by the time he met Mikey. And after that length of time, half a spliff might have been all it took to have him stumbling around like that.'

And when we finally managed to rouse him, at 11 on the Saturday morning, it seemed Mike's suspicions were right.

I'd made a full English breakfast and insisted he come down to eat with us – though reassuring him that the last thing we wanted was a row, just to talk through what had happened the previous evening. And, as we ate, I went over the facts as they'd been presented to us, telling him we were happy he'd got the train on time and met us at the arranged spot, and that we were pleased he'd found a friend in Mikey.

'But we're very disappointed,' I finished, 'to find out you'd been taking drugs. Did Mikey give them to you?'

'No comment,' he said, with a half-smile.

Which was to be expected, I supposed – the 'code', and all that.

'Well, whatever,' Mike said. 'But we trusted you, Dan. It was the very first time you'd left the house of your own volition and you went and did that. You can't believe that we'd be okay with it, surely?'

'But that's the thing, though,' Daniel said as he dipped his sausages in his egg. 'I admitted it straight away, didn't I? I didn't lie, I didn't want to. I didn't think you'd be that bothered – it's just weed, it's not like it's drugs, just weed. Everyone does it.'

'No, Dan, they don't,' I said, 'and you're not daft, I can see that. You must know that weed can be a gateway drug, surely? I assume you understand what that means?'

Daniel nodded. 'Yeah, yeah, 'course I know. Loads of people say that – it just means it can lead to bigger and better drugs.' He grinned then at both of us, fork held aloft, unconcerned. 'That's a joke, by the way. I didn't mean better drugs, obvs. But anyway, that's not me, is it?'

'I don't know, Dan,' Mike said. 'So please tell us.'

'Like, I've never done other drugs and I've done weed since junior school. It, you know, it actually helps me.'

'How?' I asked. 'How exactly do you think it helps you? Because trust me, it doesn't.'

Daniel shook his head now. 'You're wrong,' he said. 'Last night was the first night I slept good. As soon as my head hit that pillow I was totally out, bro, and I woke up feeling good.' He waggled his fork at us. 'An' *that's* because I had a joint.'

Daniel then followed up with something that truly astounded me. 'See,' he said, 'if you just got me a bit of weed each day, like, and some baccy and papers, I'd be so much better. I swear down, I'd sleep like a baby every night.'

Now it was Mike's turn to grin; it was just so ridiculous. 'Are you serious?' he said mildly. 'That's never gonna happen, mate. For one, we would lose our jobs, and for two, our grandkids come to this house, so we'd never in a million years allow any form of drugs on the premises.'

'What about if it was stashed somewhere in the back garden?' Daniel asked, ramping up the shock factor. 'Somewhere the kids couldn't reach? That'd solve that and I'd never tell the social that you let me, so you wouldn't lose your jobs.'

'It's an absolute no, Dan,' Mike said firmly, 'so forget about it. It's never going to happen and if you go off again, we don't expect you to come back in that state. And if you ever did bring anything into this house, that would be the end of it, I'm afraid.'

'You mean, I'd be off?' Dan asked, 'like, moved on again?'

'Exactly like that,' I said. 'But let's leave it there now and finish our breakfast. You know the rules, love, and we don't have many, so just think on it, okay?'

And that was that. He spent the rest of the day gaming and did the same thing on Sunday, and the drugs issue wasn't brought up again. And, weirdly, I felt all the better for it. We'd had our first frank discussion about Daniel's life before he'd come to us, and though there was still very little we really knew about him, a kind of equilibrium had been set in place. He knew where he stood and we both felt much calmer. And with an argument-free early turning off of the Wi-Fi, Mike and both slept pretty soundly. Yes, we almost certainly still had an ongoing drug situation – we weren't naive enough to suppose this would be the last of it – at least Daniel knew our red line: absolutely no drugs in the house.

By Monday lunchtime, with Daniel having skipped off to school without so much as a moan, I was feeling almost high-spirited. And with a free afternoon in prospect – I was determined to put the drugs thing out of my mind, as per Mike's mantra – I was looking forward to heading into town with Riley and spending the vouchers the kids had clubbed together to give me for my birthday. First though, I needed some clarity, so as soon as the taxi was out of sight, I was straight on the phone to Phoebe Morris.

'Oh dear,' she said, once I'd told her the state Daniel was in when we picked him up on the Friday evening. 'Well, I suppose it's to be expected – he's apparently been doing weed since he was 10 years old.'

Breaking Point

Suppose it's to be expected? It seemed a somewhat defeatist attitude, even if that was precisely what Daniel had told us.

'Yes, I know that,' I said, wondering why she didn't seem to be finding this much of an issue. 'It's all in his file and he's admitted as much to us. I was—'

'Oh, of course,' she said. 'You know all the background, don't you?' She sighed. 'I mean, I know they've been trying for years to get him off it – but they obviously haven't, have they?' Did I actually hear wry amusement in her voice as she said that? At the very least, a lack of concern about her client's drug use that I definitely didn't share.

'Clearly not,' I said, my own voice sounding much more clipped – which I think she must have picked up on, because I heard another sigh.

'Look,' she went on, 'the thing is at least doing weed is better than the hard drugs some of the kids are on, isn't it? But, no, I appreciate it's not ideal. Do you know where he got it?'

I was bemused by her apparent lack of concern about habitual weed-use in teenagers. Was this a generational thing? Perhaps she'd even used it herself. It wasn't just on the streets that recreational drug use was a thing, after all – she might well have used it at university.

'No, I don't,' I said. 'That's why I'm ringing you. Because as we've made clear to him, we will absolutely not have him bringing drugs into this house. *Any* drugs, weed included. And he obviously got it from somewhere. Presumably this kid Mikey, or someone *he* gets his weed from.'

'Oh yes, Mikey,' she said, as if the thought had only just occurred to her. I knew social workers were routinely overburdened with cases, but this was Mikey, the welcome new friend we'd discussed only three days earlier. Then she really floored me: it wasn't that she'd forgotten his name, quite the opposite.

'I've been doing a bit of digging about him,' Phoebe went on. 'Turns out he's not a new friend after all. They've met before. They were friends a couple of years ago, in fact.'

'*What*?!'

'It seems the lad was in the same children's home as Dan for a bit – after his mum had some sort of breakdown after splitting up with her partner. Not for very long, matter of only two or three months, but—'

'Long enough to make a connection with Dan, clearly. And now they're reunited and in school together. Great!'

My mind quickly collated the scant information I already had on this boy and Daniel: they were schooled in different buildings, they met up on the days that Dan went to school, so it made sense, really, that they already knew each other as it would have been odd to be able to strike up such a friendship in such a short time. Could I really have been that blinkered?

'Exactly,' Phoebe said. 'So, they were obviously, shall we say, economical with the truth.'

Breaking Point

They were indeed, I thought darkly. So much for me fretting about that Joshua character. And Daniel had lied to me. Or had he? Had he at any point told me Mikey was a 'new' friend? No, I wasn't sure he had. He'd just said he went to the same school. But Mikey's mother clearly thought they had only just become acquainted, so she'd obviously never met Daniel before. But then, if she'd been in crisis and her son temporarily in care, how much would she have known about who he was hanging out with? Either way, I wasn't comfortable with any of it.

'So, what do I say to Dan if he wants to go round there again?'

Phoebe didn't seem to need much time to consider it. 'On balance, I'd say that we allow it. I mean I *know* the drugs are an issue, of course they are, but I don't think any good will come of having him under house arrest, do you? Drugs are everywhere and he's got to learn to navigate all this stuff, after all.'

'I thought he'd already been doing exactly that, hadn't he? Navigating it all too well. Wasn't that why he came to us in the first place?'

'Yes,' she said, not seeming to hear my slightly sarcastic tone. 'But he can't be wrapped up in cotton wool, can he? Plus, as far as we know, he has never ever had a proper friend, not since he's been in care – well, undesirables excepted – and though it's turned out that it's perhaps not an ideal relationship, I think it's important we allow him to start making relationships with his peers, don't you? Kids his own age. We just have to watch over it, I suppose, and see how it goes. We can always step in if it looks like it's becoming a problem.'

So that was me told. And on one level, I did agree with her reasoning. Drugs *were* everywhere, and offered routinely to kids, so teenagers did have to learn about them. But this was a kid who, at least, according to his notes, had already been at the sharp end of the drug trade, so I wasn't sure that applied. Neither was I sure that Phoebe could *really* know that Daniel had never had a proper friend, but I supposed she knew him better than I did (and, presumably, had already 'filed' the Joshua lad into the 'undesirables' category).

So, I would have to go along with it, and would just have to be vigilant, and Mike and I would have to keep making it absolutely crystal clear to Daniel that bringing drugs into our house would be crossing a line. Even as I allowed myself to accept all of this, I knew it was adding responsibilities to my role that I hadn't expected. I was now taking care of a teenager that most of my colleagues seemed to know and accept took drugs. Not only that, the way Phoebe had just spoken to me gave me the distinct impression that this kind of thing was quite normal these days for a kid of Daniel's age. Things had certainly changed over the years, I was aware of that. Maybe I just hadn't realised how much.

But was this *really* progress? It felt way more like aiding and abetting.

Chapter 11

I should have known the watch-and-wait plan would only turn out to be temporary because, with a longer leash, Daniel soon decided to run with it. The following Thursday, having trotted off to school as planned, he didn't arrive back in the taxi as expected. The first I knew of it was when I got a call from the driver – there were a few different ones who took him to school – to say that Daniel hadn't appeared to meet his lift outside the school gates and the school themselves only knew that he had left the premises as normal. Social services weren't aware yet because the taxi company wouldn't have informed them, their duty being to let the parents know if a child didn't turn up. They did record 'no shows', but that wouldn't have been until the end of the day.

I tried calling Daniel on his mobile, but, predictably, he didn't answer and of course I hadn't even thought of adding any kind of tracker to his phone, or a 'find-my-phone' thing, whatever they were called! Since there was nothing I could do other than wait for news of some sort, I busied myself with preparing tea and then went upstairs to change the bedding in his room. Around 5 p.m., however, my mobile rang: not Daniel, as I'd hoped, but Mikey's mum, Carol.

'I'm just phoning to let you know Daniel's here,' she told me. 'He said he's sorry not to let you know, but his phone was out of battery.'

I didn't believe that for one moment. 'Well, he could have let the taxi driver know he'd changed his plans,' I said. 'Can I speak to him?'

'Oh, I didn't know he went to school by taxi,' she said. One of many things she didn't know, I thought darkly. 'Honestly, these lads. So impulsive, aren't they? But no, sorry – I just said I'd let you know he's safe with me while they've popped down the chippy to get some tea. Shall I have him call you when they get back? Though, really, please don't worry. Once they're fed and they've had a chance to play whatever stupid game all the kids are currently obsessed by, I'll be sure to get him on the 8.45 train for you – it's no bother.'

I pondered insisting that Daniel call me himself but, really, what was the point? If she was definitely putting him on the train – and presumably by then his apparently dead phone was going to have some charge in it – he could text me to confirm that he needed picking up from the station.

'I'll have him do that then,' she said, when I told her that would be fine. 'Lads, eh? Who'd have 'em?'

Breaking Point

I ended the call, feeling cross but, once again, impotent. Though I had no reason to suppose Carol was anything other than a normal busy mum, firefighting all the usual teenaged shenanigans, I had the familiar nagging sense that we were both being taken for mugs. I pondered calling back and bringing up the weed situation, but stayed my hand; she either knew about the drugs and was turning a blind eye to it, or, potentially, it wasn't even anything to do with Mikey. Unlikely, I thought, but there was still the possibility that Daniel had got hold of the drugs that night from another source.

There was also the small matter of Daniel breezily ignoring the taxi that had been booked for him and all the inconvenience that had caused. But, once again, there was nothing I could do but wait until I heard from him.

And, at 20 to nine, when my mobile trilled again, I assumed it must be Daniel to let me know – presumably pretty sheepishly – that he was indeed waiting on the platform for the quarter to nine train.

It wasn't Daniel, however: it was Carol once again.

'They went out after tea,' she explained, 'but they haven't come back. And Mikey's phone is now off too. And now it's too late to make the train. Little buggers!' She laughed indulgently. 'The last one's at 10. Shall I put him on that one instead?'

There was little to say other than yes.

'But where did they go?' I asked. 'Do you know?'

'Down to the park, I imagine. A lot of local kids like to hang out there. I'm sure they'll be back soon – probably just lost track of time. I'll keep you posted.'

'Just one more thing,' I said quickly, as the thought had been nagging at me, 'I don't want to get anyone into trouble here, but does Mikey smoke weed?'

Carol laughed. 'Is the Pope Catholic?' she asked. 'Yes, he does. Not like all the time, you understand, just now and again.

'I don't go mad about it,' she added. 'They all do it, don't they?'

I wasn't quite sure how to answer that, because the true answer wasn't 'yes, they do', but 'no'. I just fudged it, sighing heavily and saying, 'Well, it seems to be going that way, doesn't it?' Then quickly added that it would indeed be good if she kept me posted.

I ended the call both saddened and surprised by what Carol had said. Was doing weed really so commonplace these days that parents thought it was funny to even be asked about it?

'So, what do I do now?' I asked Mike, who'd paused the TV and come across to hear the latest. 'Should I phone the Emergency Duty Team or the police and report him missing, or should I wait till 10 to see if Carol gets him on that train?'

'Well, I reckon that if you call the police now, they'll only tell you that you should leave it till after 10 anyway, so why don't we wait and see? Or rather,' he added, reading my mind, 'wait till he's *not* on the 10 o'clock train.' He frowned. 'Because, much as I wish otherwise, I'm having a bit of a "you" moment – something tells me he won't be.'

'Plan,' I agreed. 'And in the meantime, I'm going to email Phoebe and Christine to let them know what's going on.'

I pulled out my laptop and did exactly that. Even if neither saw the message until the morning, this sort of thing all needed documenting. And once that was done, I called Carol, not expecting her to tell me they had miraculously appeared, because she'd have called me if that were the case, but to let her know what I now had to do.

As expected, there had been no further sign of them. 'And, trust me, I'll wring my lad's neck when I get hold of him,' she told me.

'I'm sure you will,' I agreed. 'But I wanted to let you know that I now have a duty to call the police and report Daniel missing.'

I could hear her sharp intake of breath. 'The *police*?' she said, sounding even more anxious now. 'Do you have to? I mean they *will* turn up eventually, and no matter what time it is, I'll put them to bed. Dan can stay here tonight and I'll send him back to you tomorrow.'

'I'm really sorry,' I told her, 'but as I said, I have a duty to ring them and the Emergency Duty Team too. But if they *do* turn up, can you please ring me straight away? It doesn't matter what time it is, even if it's in the middle of the night, as the police will need to be told.

It's not like either of us is going to get much sleep until we know where they are, is it?'

Carol agreed, albeit very reluctantly – she was obviously nervous about involving the police or social services and I got that. But I also knew in my bones that this was more than two lads having larks in the park. I then went through all the rigmarole of ringing EDT and then the police, giving descriptions of Daniel and the clothes he'd been wearing, and, with the police, also pointing out his history with drugs and drug dealers, and letting them know he was used to being out on the streets.

There was little else to do then, other than head up to bed, taking our sense of impending doom, of all the small gains we thought we'd made beginning to fall away, with us. Which obviously didn't encourage restful sleep. Plus, I still couldn't access what had always been my go-to; that ability I thought I'd always had to see my way past the difficult behaviours, the deceit, the abusive language, the aggression, the unwillingness to connect to the vulnerable child with the terrible past who is actually crying out for help and understanding. Why couldn't I do so here? Because with Daniel, all I felt was anger and frustration. Why?

I finally succumbed to exhaustion at around 3 a.m., and still no word from anyone regarding Daniel's whereabouts.

Chapter 12

By some miracle, I must have fallen into a really deep sleep because when my mobile began trilling at me, it was a while before it dawned on me that it wasn't happening in my dream – which was a very different place, and definitely a much nicer one. So, I was still groggy when my fumbling hand found the phone on my bedside table. When I picked it up, it resisted, so there was another bout of fumbling as I sought to release it from its charging cord.

It was 6.30 a.m., still not quite light. Realising that Mike was now spark out beside me, I threw the covers off and scuttled out onto the landing before answering – I knew who it probably was, and they obviously knew to wait. And with his alarm due to go off in less than half an hour now, I knew my husband needed all the shut-eye he could get.

'Hi,' I said, pulling the bedroom door closed behind me. 'Is there news?'

'There is indeed,' the duty officer said, after introducing himself. 'We have him in custody. We caught him and Mikey on stolen bikes at about four this morning. They were both off their heads on something, but, surprise, surprise, they refused to say what. Just that they'd been given some pills. Anyway, they've slept it off some – which is why I didn't see any point in calling you earlier—'

'For which I'm really, really grateful,' I told him, as I hurried down the stairs.

He chuckled. 'No sense in us both being up, is there? Plus, I get to go home to bed in – let me see – less than two hours now, whereas you –' again, the wry chuckle; I liked this man immediately '– have to deal with me laddos. Well, one of them, at any rate. Mikey's mother's on her way to collect him now.'

'So where did you find them?' I asked, making my way to the kitchen.

He named a park – one that was way over the other side of town from us and also a long way from Mikey's house. One where they definitely hadn't been playing on the swings.

'Wow,' I said, 'how did they get all the way over *there*?'

'On those stolen bikes I mentioned. Stolen from two different addresses. Then they just pedalled around, leading us on a not-very-merry dance. Still, all's well – we've at least managed to establish the bikes' owners.'

'I'm glad to hear it. I'll get down to pick Daniel up as soon as I can.'

Breaking Point

'No rush, Mrs Watson. You take your time, okay? Go back to bed for a bit, if you want to. It's not as if he's going anywhere, is he?'

I obviously wouldn't be doing that – now I was awake, there was no way I'd manage to go back to sleep again. Plus, with Mike needing to get off to work, it didn't feel right to anyway. So, grateful as I was for the officer's kind suggestion, I decided I might as well shower, fuel up with a bucket of strong coffee, then drive down to the police station and face the music. Or rather, I corrected myself, make sure *Daniel* did.

Some 15 years previously – could it really have been that long ago? – I had driven to the same police station and parked up outside, following a call from my then fostering supervisor, John Fulshaw, who was in a bit of a bind over an 11-year-old lad. He'd been taken into custody after allegedly stabbing his stepmother, for whom (perhaps understandably, I'd thought at the time) it had been the proverbial straw that broke the camel's back. No way was she having him home again, *ever*, and yes, she would most definitely be pressing charges.

I'd rocked up in the middle of an already stressful day, having left my dad getting gowned up for bowel surgery. And though, logically, I knew it should all be straightforward, having to try and stop my mum from manically catastrophising was now affecting me too, so going down to meet this lad, who was apparently raging, was as much of a distraction as anything else.

There was also something about the few facts I knew that drew me in. Just 11, no other family, lived with Dad plus his 'wicked' stepmother, younger half-brother – beloved son of aforementioned dad and step-mum, and absolutely nowhere to go – well, it all had such a compelling Cinderella vibe, I simply couldn't *not* go and meet him.

And they'd been right – he *was* raging. When I'd got there, he was busy kicking chairs around and swearing like a navvy, and acknowledged my arrival with a snarl and 'who the fuck is she?' But despite the attitude, the earlier knife-wielding and his constant lashing out, there was something about the boy that couldn't help but grip my heart. It made me realise, if somewhat cheesily (it had been an emotional kind of morning), that helping him was exactly what I'd been put on Earth to do.

So, we'd taken him in and also taken on a challenge of supporting this lad, who had had one of the saddest, saddest starts in life, in the long, complicated business of becoming the young man Mike and I both truly believed he had it in him to be.

That boy was Tyler, now our beloved son in all but biology, and agreeing to take him in was one of the best snap decisions I think I had ever made. Which made me think, as I parked up and undid my seat belt. Daniel too had been 11 when he found himself abandoned, but unlike Tyler, there had been no foster family willing or free to take him in. And for Daniel, like Tyler, this had been a 'sliding doors' moment. Where might Tyler be now, had his luck then been different? Where might Daniel be now, too? I must, I decided, as I walked towards the station, keep that 11-year-old boy firmly imprinted in my mind.

It was after eight now, the working day for most just beginning, but the officer I'd spoken to looked just as tired as I'd imagined, and keen, no doubt, to get home to bed. Mikey and his mum, he told me, had left over an hour ago – which suited me, because I didn't want to conduct a post-mortem with her right now – leaving Daniel the only person currently in the cells. 'And asleep,' he added. 'You might have a job waking him, to be honest. But, come along, let's see if we can put enough of a rocket under him that you can get him in your car and get him home.'

Daniel was, in fact, stirring when we got to his cell – well, if sitting on the edge of your bed, head in hands, rocking, could strictly be given that name. He looked a mess; unkempt, dirty, his hair lank and greasy. In fact, he looked exactly as anyone would expect him to look – a lad who'd been up all night, running amok and taking drugs. And definitely not a spliff. Well, he might have had one – he probably had, I reasoned – but other drugs too, those as yet unknown pills.

'Dan,' I said. 'Come on, let's get you home.'

To which his only response was to groan.

'Come on, me laddo,' said the duty officer, kindness evident in his voice despite his obvious exhaustion. 'Let's get you out of here. Back to your own bed, yes?

'I'll give you a hand, Mrs Watson,' he added, crossing the small space to place an arm around Daniel's back, so that he could support him under his armpit. 'Sooner you're out of here, sooner I can get home to bed myself.'

Floppy and acquiescent, Daniel simply let himself be lifted and I was grateful for the help as he was obviously unsteady on his feet and I doubted I'd be able to manage him on my own. I looped an arm around his other elbow, and, together, we shuffled out, my nostrils prickling at the pungent smell of stale body odour – I guessed riding around the streets all night, with the police giving chase, probably meant he'd worked up quite a sweat.

It was a smell that only intensified once we were both finally in the car and belted up. I'd put him in the back – given the state of him, I really didn't want him riding next to me – and as we drove away, I could see him in the rear-view mirror: dark stubble, a sheen of moisture across his forehead and nose, and a distinct greyish pallor.

'Do you feel sick?' I asked. 'Because if you do, be sure to tell me, okay?' I reached into the doorwell and pulled out one of the carrier bags I habitually kept there. 'And take this,' I told him, handing the bag to him. 'I can pull over, but keep a hold of it just in case.'

He shook his head. 'I'm done spewing,' he mumbled, but still reached a hand out to take it, before slumping back in the seat again and closing his eyes. 'I just need my pit, yeah?'

'Dan,' I went on, 'what exactly *did* you take? It's important that you tell me. It might be something that—'

'Just *pills*,' he muttered, his eyes still firmly closed. 'I just need to sleep it off, yeah? I'm done, need my pit.'

With the rush hour in full swing now, it would be a while yet before that happy state of affairs came to pass, I realised, but there was little to be gained in saying so.

'And you will,' I said, still figuring that even if he had nothing to say, I certainly did. 'But once you have slept it off, whatever *it* is, you and I are going to need to have a serious talk. You've caused a lot of people a lot of stress and hassle. And—'

'Oh my *days*! I don't *need* this,' Daniel wailed suddenly. And glancing back, I could see his face was contorted, his chin quivering. He really was in a very bad way. '*Please*, just let me sleep, I *beg* you. I don't *know* what the pills were, okay? Some roadman gave us them – just sent us wild for a bit, like a buzz, just a buzz, and that's *it*!'

Thanks to my teenage grandson, Levi, and his hysterical penchant for looking up urban slang and trying to use it to make us laugh, I did know what a 'roadman' was. A young man who dressed in a certain way – tracksuit, white trainers, cap and black puffer jacket usually – and prone to cycling around, dealing drugs.

There was no point in continuing this conversation, I realised, until whatever *this* drug was had left Daniel's system. But as I drove, I kept glancing back at him, anxiously checking there was no deterioration. It soon seemed clear that he was deeply asleep again. I'd dealt with plenty of hungover teens in my time, so nothing new there, but as he slept, it occurred to me just how little he looked like a 15-year-old boy now; he put me more in mind of some addled old drunk who'd been slung out of a pub. Which was unfair of me, I reminded myself – he couldn't help his build or his stubble. But what struck me most was that, hard as I tried to bring it to mind – and I really did – I simply could not see that abandoned 11-year-old I'd read about.

Putting Daniel to bed proved to be less of a challenge than I'd anticipated. Once he'd staggered out of the car, he pretty much got himself indoors and up the stairs, seemingly propelled by the understanding that his bed wasn't far away now, which had clearly given him a sudden burst of energy. I duly followed, but once up there, it was clear I was redundant. He crawled into bed fully clothed and pulled the duvet over his head, so having run down and brought him back a pint glass of water, I left him to it – to literally stew in his own juices. For now, there seemed little else I could do.

Other than make some phone calls, that was.

The first was to Christine.

'I'm so sorry, Casey,' she said after listening to me pour my heart out, 'and I know this might sound lame, given your last 24 hours, but really, I am. Is there anything I can do?'

'Well, it's not sympathy I need, Chris,' I said, 'not if I'm honest. In fact, I'm seriously considering if we've made a huge mistake here. This doesn't feel like I'm caring for this kid at all. It feels more like containment and that's not what we signed up for.'

'I absolutely understand,' Christine said, 'and it doesn't surprise me at all that you feel like giving up. All I can ask is that you sleep on it and see how you feel in the morning. Just give it a little bit longer. I know I shouldn't be asking that, and I'm aware that we all made the same promise to you that we'd pull this placement if you felt that it wasn't working, and we will if that's the case, you have my word on that. I just feel that you're doing wonders for this kid, even if it doesn't look like that right now.'

'No, it doesn't,' I agreed flatly.

'Maybe because you're so close to it? Anyway, what do you say? At least worth sleeping on?'

'Okay, let me do that,' I said, realising I still had a whole day to get through before the sanctuary of my own bed. 'I need to phone Phoebe now. Let's see what she has to say.'

'We're all on the same team here,' Christine said mildly, clearly having misinterpreted my meaning.

'I know, Chris,' I said, dredging a wry chuckle from somewhere. 'Just not sure I have the stamina for being told how well everything's going – again.'

Which was, of course, what happened. Because it seemed Phoebe was singing from the same hymn sheet. Or, as was increasingly my impression with this placement, consulting a tick-list of steps to be taken and marking them off one by one. And the latest one, perhaps predictably, was the 'stepping in' she had alluded to in the conversation we'd had before Daniel had gone AWOL and been returned to us during the comedown from what had obviously been a cocktail of illegal chemicals.

'I'm thinking we need to get him set up with a substance abuse counsellor,' she said, once I'd again run through the events of the last few hours and voiced my doubts that we were making much headway. And rather quickly, to my mind, as if she'd already made up her mind that this was the ideal solution – which she clearly thought it was. 'Anyway, leave it with me,' she added. 'I'll get onto that right away.'

'But surely you've been down this road already?' I asked her, thinking this all seemed more like a way to keep us on side than done with any conviction that it would make any difference.

'Well, yes, it's on his record that there have been various attempts made, you're right. But it was always difficult to ensure Dan engaged with it while he was in the children's home. It was more of a group thing – two or three of the kids, from what I can gather – so I'm guessing more messing around than listening. But now he's in a home environment, you know, with you and your husband supporting him, ensuring he attends any appointments we manage to set up, either in the home or elsewhere, it just might work.'

I was about to suggest that, to my mind, it was probably going to be a waste of time this time as well, when Phoebe went on to admit, almost as if reading my mind now, that this was even though she personally doubted it would work. 'But, I mean, we have to keep trying,' she added. 'Keep chipping away. I mean, what else *can* we do?'

Much as I was feeling irritated by this apparent box-ticking – would she be quite as matter-of-fact about it all if she was the one living with Daniel? – I had to concede that this was exactly where we were at. We had to do something; it was right there in the term for his status as a child being cared for by social services. He was 'in care'. So, he had to be cared for. A 'looked-after child' who the law required had to be looked after. And looking after a child involved plugging away to try and make things better. Not, as I had pointed out to Christine earlier, simply containing them and keeping them safe. Just because such interventions hadn't worked before wasn't a valid reason for them not to be tried again. I felt suddenly chastened, as if this young social worker was Jiminy Cricket sitting on my shoulder and reminding me of things I should have instinctively known. It was no different, really, to those early years of parenthood, when toddlers were 'tamed' not by divine intervention, but by the determination and commitment of tired, frustrated parents, tantrum by soul-sapping tantrum.

Well, it was a bit different, obviously. Years of abuse and neglect, followed by a complete absence of love and security, meant that even getting Daniel to accept that help was needed felt, to everyone, I was sure, like a herculean task.

'You're right,' I conceded. 'We do have to keep trying.'

'And you never know,' she added brightly, 'if it's with the right person, at the right time ... you know, miracles can happen!'

Perhaps I'd been wrong about Phoebe seeming defeatist. Was it actually sheer dogged optimism that kept her doing what she did? If so, I wished I shared her mindset.

'I suppose they do,' I said, exhaustion beginning to seep into my brain now. 'But I have to tell you, Phoebe, Mike and I have been talking. I've just spoken to Christine and told her the same; I'm really struggling with this placement. I honestly feel we're not getting anywhere with Dan – he doesn't seem to want any kind of relationship with us and I'm beginning to feel – well, have felt from pretty early on, if I'm honest with you – that he sees our home as little more than a place to eat and sleep, while he carries on just as he always has. How can we help him if he categorically doesn't want us to?'

'Oh,' she said, sounding shocked at this revelation. 'But look how far he's come!'

Breaking Point

Had my mouth not already been open while I tried to stifle a yawn, it definitely would have been now.

'How?' I said, now genuinely keen to hear what she had to say. She'd obviously given Christine a positive picture, but I wanted to hear exactly what had prompted her to do so. 'In what way?'

'Well, you've got him back into education for the first time in ages. That's incredible. You've also given him the opportunity to bond with a friend. Yes, albeit a dodgy one, as it turns out – I'll give you that, ha ha – but a friend all the same, which is a *huge* sea-change for Daniel. You've given him trust to go off on his own. You've got him to accept boundaries, such as the early Wi-Fi turn off. Honestly, Casey, everyone who knows him, and a lot of us do, cannot *believe* all the changes in him. And I mean, at least from what I can see, he actually seems happy!'

'*Happy?*' I said to Mike, who'd called for an update almost the very moment my call with Phoebe ended – the social worker heading off to presumably congratulate herself on being able to point out how much progress had been made and me to shake my head in bemusement. 'I mean, *seriously?*' I rolled my eyes heavenward, even though Mike couldn't see it. 'Does that child seem happy to *you?*'

'Happy that he can run rings round us,' Mike observed wryly. 'But –' he paused. 'You know, maybe she does have a point, love. Those things are all true and they do constitute progress, I suppose. Perhaps we're just so close to it all that we can't see it ourselves. We don't know what he was like before he came to us, do we?'

I had to admit this was true. 'So, what do I tell Christine? She's been pushing hard for us to hang in there a bit longer. So, do we commit to another month? And don't say it's my call,' I added, poking a finger into his chest. 'Team decision.'

'Well, if this drug counselling thing gets set up, I suppose that's another bit of support we'll have with him. And, if he starts going into school every day, there'll be more routine in his life and less opportunity to get up to mischief. Shall we give it the month? What do *you* think?'

'I don't *know* what I think!' I wailed, perhaps a touch melodramatically. 'Actually,' I added, regrouping mentally, 'that's not true. What I actually think is that if I give up on him now, just when everyone is telling me he's making progress, I'll just feel awful about it. I'll feel so guilty even though I'm not sure I *am* feeling that right now, not in my bones. No, you're right,' I finished. 'Let's see how we go with school and if the counselling makes any difference. I'll tell Christine yes and make her day. And on our own heads be it, eh?'

That decided, I called my manager and informed her that I didn't need to sleep on it and after much deliberation we'd decided to try another month and see how it went.

'We do want you to push hard for more days at school though,' I added. 'That would make our lives so much easier, as well as giving some much-needed structure to Dan.'

Christine promised she'd try her hardest to swing that and thanked me profusely for 'saving the day', which of course made me smile. I was well used to such flowery compliments from social workers and managers by now and I did wonder if they must take a course in such niceties as part of their training. I could practically see it playing out, with some instructor standing in front of a whiteboard, pointing out 'when all else fails phrases' such as: 'You really are a star!', 'You've done so much more than we could hope for!', 'You've worked miracles, you really have!' And then of course the one I was currently falling for, 'Just try to hold on for a little longer, we know you can do it!'

Horrible to realise it, but was I finally becoming cynical?

Chapter 13

It was 4 p.m. before I decided it was time for Daniel and I to have our 'debrief'. By this time, he'd had his loud rap music blaring down through the bedroom floor for a good half-hour, so I knew he was definitely awake. I'd yet to hear the shower though, so that was high on the agenda, and definitely before Mike got home and we thought about tea.

In fact, all I could think about was that we had agreed to keep going and I was suffering from a big bout of buyer's remorse. *You're just tired*, I told myself, as I trudged up the stairs. *It will all feel much better once you've slept*.

I didn't bother knocking on the door when I went up because I knew there was no way Daniel would hear me. Instead, I opened it and walked straight into the room, where my nose told me immediately that I'd probably – no, almost *definitely* – made the wrong call with Christine. The stench of cannabis was so strong, I was genuinely surprised that I hadn't picked it up already from downstairs.

And there was Daniel himself, leaning out of the window and smoking a joint, either oblivious to the fact, or not even caring, that anyone walking past the house could see him. Or that I would almost certainly find out. And this after we had spelled out to him, so very clearly and so often, that he was never to bring drugs into our house. And this – I was almost spitting with fury now – after I'd picked him up only hours before from a police station, on a comedown from bloody drugs, having been awake half the night!

The sheer audacity, the cheek of it, the total lack of respect made my hackles immediately rise. It also infuriated me that this had been happening even as Christine and then Phoebe had been singing his – and our – praises, convincing me that it was negative of me not to give him the benefit of the doubt about this little hiccup and keep plugging away for a bit longer. It was like he was laughing in my face.

'Put that out *right now*,' I demanded, striding over to him.

He turned and grinned at me; actually *grinned* at me – he was clearly feeling much better after the luxury of sleeping the day away. 'I ain't fucking throwing it,' he drawled, mid-smoky exhale. 'I had to sell loads of shit last night to get this.'

I was so livid that I acted before responding – I simply snatched it from his hand and hurled it through the open window. Which at least had the effect of rendering him speechless. His pupils, I noticed, were like black holes. He was out of it again, clearly, and I was out of patience.

I planted a hand on each hip. 'You know, Dan,' I told him, 'I don't actually care that you smoke weed. It is what it is, and you're obviously addicted to the stuff.'

This offended him, as it had been designed to.

'No, I'm not!' he squeaked indignantly.

I didn't grace that nonsense with an answer – I'd leave that to the substance abuse counsellor Phoebe was probably trying to get organised even as I breathed in the stench of the cannabis.

'Whatever,' I said, exasperated. 'Maybe you do it because you think it gives you some kind of status, then. But you know the score: you will *not* bring that crap into my house, you hear me? And I cannot believe you even did that, given the events of last night.'

To my surprise, he immediately put two hands up in supplication. 'Okay, okay, I hear you. Sorry. I'm *sorry*. Can I smoke it in the garden instead, then?'

I sighed heavily. What *were* we going to do with him? Now that I was ready for a showdown, to reinforce those all-important boundaries, he wasn't even being confrontational. Quite the opposite, just matter of fact. He'd been busted and he was sorry. No biggie. But of course he was. Because to him, I realised, this really *was* nothing very much, despite Mike and I having already had this conversation with him. A minor transgression.

Breaking Point

A little bit of teenage mischief that was probably par for the course back in the children's home. A 'rap on the knuckles and business as usual' kind of mischief, and as for last night, that was clearly ancient history.

'I mean, like the *back* garden, obvs,' he added, with a watery smile – or what he plainly thought would be an appeasing, win-me-over, goofy one. Which put me in mind of the silly picture his friend Bella had shown me of him when she'd been briefly staying with us. It was the weirdest kind of circumstance – this hulking kid smoking a spliff in my house – but for some reason it made me glimpse the vulnerable child beneath all the facial hair.

It hit me forcibly then: he really was just a kid. I could feel my initial welling of anger start to dissipate a little as I looked at him. Despite his height, and bulk and attitude, he *was* still a kid – a messed-up kid. A kid, I reminded myself, who'd *been* messed up. And I needed to keep reminding myself of that fact every time anger threatened to overcome me.

And he was now looking up at me hopefully, I realised, as if we could have a reasonable conversation about just where he could and couldn't smoke. So perhaps that was exactly what we should have.

I sat down on his bed and sighed.

'I'm afraid not, Dan,' I said. 'You already know I can't allow that – and why. So, no, not in the front garden *or* the back garden. I'll never be okay with it, wherever you end up doing it. But here? In mine and Mike's *house*?

What were you even thinking after everything we've said to you, or do you just have no respect for us at all?'

He came and joined me on the bed, sitting down with a whump.

'I know,' he said quietly. 'I know I shouldn'ta.'

'Well, now it's gone.' And was hopefully not burning a hole in my grass. 'And I'm really hoping this will be the last of it. Was it just the one joint you had?'

He nodded. 'Yeah.'

'And where did you get it from? The "roadman"?'

He looked aghast. 'I can't tell you stuff like that!'

'That's exactly what you told me this morning. Or did you forget? And how did you pay for it, given that you didn't have any money?'

'We didn't have to pay.'

'We?'

'Me and Mikey, we both got given one.'

And the police had obviously, I thought angrily, failed to find them when they searched the boys – at least Daniel's one, anyway. How had he managed to pull that off? But it was a pointless line of enquiry, so I didn't bother pursuing it.

'So, they were given to you,' I said instead. 'Why would anyone just give you two joints?'

'Why d'you think?' There was an edge of irritation in his voice, the response automatic. But then there was a shift in the body language – something I'd not seen before. I don't know if it was the effect of the joint, or just him being too tired for sparring, but he turned to face me, his expression now almost apologetic. I could smell his musky blokey body spray, mingled with old sweat. He needed that shower. A good hairwash. To change into freshly washed clothes. Some purpose and direction beyond this pointless existence.

'I think I can guess, Dan,' I answered. 'But how about you tell me anyway?'

'I mean – sorry, I mean for, like, selling drugs, obviously. That's why we stole the bikes. So we could get over to my old patch a bit quicker.'

I had already worked out that the school Daniel attended was only about three quarters of an hour's walk from his former children's home and that the possibility of him hooking up with his friends there was always present. But there was no getting around that, since it was the only local school that would take him. I thought about Mikey; I wondered what kind of conversation he and his mother would be having right now and made a mental note that I should probably try and speak to her.

'To sell the drugs there, I'm guessing? Like you used to.'

Another nod.

'For which you were going to get paid, yes?'

'Yeah,' he said. 'At the weekend. The joints were, like, subs.'

I remembered the state he'd been in when I'd collected him. '*Just* the joints?'

'And some pills, like. You know, just to keep us going.'

'What pills? What kind of pills?'

He shrugged. 'I dunno. Just, you know, pills.'

'The same as you took before?'

He shrugged. 'Guess so.'

Such astounding naivety. I wondered if there would ever be a time when conversations of this nature didn't feel deeply, deeply troubling. Yes, I knew drug taking was endemic in some parts of society and that teenagers in particular were risk-takers because their brains were not yet fully formed. So, yes, I knew the science, but it still appalled me to think that a child could accept, almost without question, a 'bunch of pills' from someone they already knew broke the law. Pills that could be anything. But accepted with such blind faith.

'All of which you've now taken?'

'Yeah, 'course. Like I said, they were to keep us going.'

Going about the business, I thought angrily, of lining drug dealers' pockets. But which dealers? Much as I wished it, I knew he'd never tell me. But there was no point in this conversation turning into that kind of conversation anyway. He'd opened up to me, which at least *did* feel something like the progress Phoebe had raved about. Only a modicum, admittedly, but progress even so. It was the first time we'd had a conversation about something emotive or challenging that didn't involve sass and confrontation. But, as it turned out, it was all the progress we'd be making today.

'Well, love,' I told him, 'you know this has to stop now. I need to keep you safe, so that means no more going round to Mikey's, I'm afraid.'

Breaking Point

Daniel shook his head. Then he sighed, almost as if he were the disappointed parent and I was the errant teenager who needed putting straight.

'I'm not being funny, Casey,' he said mildly, 'so don't take this the wrong way, okay, because I don't mean nothing by it. But you and Mike can't stop me. Okay, so I won't bring drugs or weed back here. That's fair enough. But I can jump a train to Mikey's if you won't give me the fare. Either way, I'll be going over later. But I swear I'll come back on the eight-thirty train – I can't be arsed freezing my tits off all night again tonight.'

It was, no question, a pretty astounding string of words. And delivered, despite the weed, in such a measured and articulate way that it had the effect of rendering me almost speechless. But, at the same time, I knew everything he'd just kindly explained to me was true. He'd even popped in the bit about which train he'd be on, so no need for me to go through the rigmarole of calling EDT – assuming he came good on that, and I suspected he would, for the reason he'd already given me: he really did hold all the cards.

Except one.

'Daniel,' I said, 'we've spoken several times about actions and consequences. Yes, you're right, I can't physically stop you leaving the house. But neither can Mike and I help you move forward, or onto a better path, if you won't engage with us and accept the boundaries you've been given. Given for *your* benefit, remember? Seriously. Don't you *want* to make a better life for yourself, get away from the criminality? You'll be 16 soon. You surely have *some* hopes and dreams. And you know, love, being here with us – that's what it's all about, helping you find a path towards them.'

Daniel stared into space for a moment, as if weighing up possible futures he might choose for himself. ''Course I got dreams,' he said, finally. And for a moment, I thought I might gain some insight, however tiny, into what made him tick, who he was. But he slapped his hands down on his knees and then abruptly stood up. 'But you know how it is,' he added, raising his arms and stretching to reveal his pale, still-youthful torso. 'Right now, I gotta work, end of.'

I stood up too. 'But you *don't*, Daniel. You can leave all this behind you, you do not *have* to do this.'

He shook his head, almost sadly. 'No. Trust me, I do.'

Despite all the years of fostering I had under my belt, I don't think I'd ever felt such a stark sense of powerlessness as I did when I left that bedroom. And, as I went back downstairs, any thought of making food for Daniel now forgotten, I was horrified by the insane, frankly astonishing situation we were in. I had a 15-year-old child under my roof who had not only confessed to stealing, to drug-taking, and to selling drugs, to boot, but who was now prepared to go out and do at least one of those things again, if not all. And since I now knew all about it, wasn't I complicit if I did nothing to stop him? *The law*, I thought, *sometimes is an ass*.

Breaking Point

It was already beginning to get dark and rain was falling steadily. But heavily enough to make Daniel reconsider his plan of action? Somehow, given the relaxed tone in which he'd spelled his position out to me, I doubted it. He had decided what he was doing and had made it clear that I was powerless to stand in his way. But my sense that there needed to be *something* done in opposition to him was very strong. Even if I couldn't physically, or legally, stop him from walking out of our front door, he did need to know that as someone who was charged with taking care of children who'd had the worst starts in life, and with supporting them and nurturing them, every fibre of my being was strenuously opposed to it. It was mine and Mike's job to give him the tools to try and change his life's course and we took the responsibility seriously. He had been placed with us with the intention of getting him away from drug dealers' clutches, and, so far, we had totally failed in that task. Worse still, at that moment, while I waited impatiently for my coffee machine to play its part in shoring me up mentally, I couldn't see how anything would change – all Mike and I seemed to represent was a change in Daniel's location and a bunch of attendant logistical challenges to be overcome.

Was this really where we were at? At the very least, I felt the need for a second opinion. I went into our little snug, closed the door and called Phoebe again.

'All you can do,' she said, once I'd outlined our current impasse, 'is reiterate your position. That he's in your care, he's a minor and that you do not give your permission for him to leave the house right now. It doesn't actually matter that you know where he's going and what he's going to be doing. The same applies if he changes tack and says he's off to the chip shop or the skate park instead. Just tell him no, that he's grounded. Oh, and I'm assuming he's already had his pocket money for this week?'

'Yes.'

'Then obviously do not give him any more money.'

'Even though he's already told me he'll fare-dodge if I don't? That feels almost as if I'm encouraging him to commit a crime.'

'I know, but that's clearly not the case. In fact, the opposite is true. If you give him money, you are actively helping him, aren't you? No, you are just playing it by the book, which is all you can do. And if he still leaves the house—'

'Which he will, absolutely no question—'

'Give it till 10 p.m. and then ring the police and report him missing again. We have to keep doing our bit even if he won't do his.'

But to what end? I thought as we ended the call, my calm rationalisation of earlier long gone now. This placement felt as if it was turning into a slow-motion car crash – a feeling that only intensified when I emerged from the snug to find Daniel in the kitchen. He'd obviously just showered; his hair was damp and he was wearing just a pair of gym shorts and slides, and was now, apparently, looking for me.

'Oh, there you are,' he said amiably. 'Any chance of a couple of rounds of sandwiches or something? One for now, like, and maybe one for the journey?'

This wasn't just a slow-motion car crash, I realised, as I went over to the bread bin. It was a slow-motion car crash accessorised by a bloody picnic. Made by me. Because what else could I do but feed him?

Chapter 14

True to his word, Daniel left the house around 5 p.m. I dutifully went through the script Phoebe had given me, which felt utterly pointless, since his response, having stood there politely and listened to it (some of Phoebe's precious progress in action, I grudgingly conceded), was to shrug his coat on, flip his hood up, thread his arms through the straps of his backpack, then say 'noted', following it with a grinning thumbs-up, presumably for my being word perfect. And as I watched him from the doorstep – I stayed there until he was out of sight – it occurred to me that perhaps this was no more or less than what I should have expected. What did he know of family, of adults caring whether he came home or not? Of people who felt affection for him, felt love for him? Very little, if anything. And me making him two rounds of sandwiches hardly changed that.

What I *could* do, I decided, was speak to Carol. But her phone went straight to voicemail, so I could only

Breaking Point

leave a message, to let her know Daniel was on his way to meet Mikey, and to suggest that we talk.

By the time Mike came home, however, I had heard nothing back from her, and I was by now so mired in matters psychological and philosophical that the first thing I did when he arrived was to quote attachment theory at him, plus my own theory, which had become more certain by the hour, that if Daniel was as happy as Phoebe had suggested, it wasn't because of the supposed progress we were making, but because he was back in the place that suited him best – answering to no one and doing pretty much what he liked. At least to *his* mind.

In reality, this was far from the truth. What was happening here wasn't even about Daniel. It was us – me and Mike – in battle with the drug dealers, who were, little by little, reclaiming ownership of him. I felt so out of my depth that I was on the verge of ringing the police right there and then, and telling them everything I knew.

'But what exactly is that, Case?' Mike asked. 'Who does he go to see other than Mikey? We don't know. Which dealers are having him run around for them? We don't know. What drugs exactly is he involved with? We don't know that either. Let's give it some time – have our tea, watch a bit of telly or something. If he doesn't turn up, well then, we know the procedure. But this time, we'll call it in, do our job and then go to bed and try and forget about it. Remember what I said about how we react? When we can't change what's happening, we can certainly change how we react to it.'

'That's easier said than done!' I snapped, getting irritated about the fact that I seemed to be the only one who was irritated. 'If the bloody school get wind of this, they might sling him out, let alone give him the four days he's meant to be now getting when they go back after half term.'

The school had broken up for the holidays now, but Phoebe had emailed me to say they'd found an extra slot for Daniel. Next week, when they returned, he would be going every day apart from Mondays. I walked off to the kitchen in a huff to check on the pork chops that I'd left sizzling in the oven. Mike followed me through after hanging his coat in the hall.

'School won't be bothered, love,' he said. 'What he does on the outside won't concern them.'

I must have been compartmentalising so many different emotions – so that they didn't overwhelm me – that Mike's soothing tone, and his arm around my waist, opened up my internal release valve. Just like that, it all came flooding out.

'Mike, I've just sat and listened to a boy – a child really – tell me that he's going out dealing drugs for God knows who, that he smokes dope and pops pills, that somehow he has no choice but to do all this, and he was smiling at me while he said it all.' I was really crying now and almost hysterical as I clung to him. 'And he thought it was all so normal, and I, I don't know, it almost *sounded* bloody normal to me! I mean, what's all that about?'

Breaking Point

Mike hugged me, saying nothing, until I finally stopped crying, then pulled away to reach for some kitchen roll so I could blow my nose. He then led me across to the dining table and pulled out a chair.

'Let's just sit for a minute, Case,' he said, before sitting down himself. He then put his head into his hands, his fingers messing up his hair – an action I'd only seen him do a handful of times, all of which had been deeply stressful. 'You're right,' he finally said, 'you're absolutely right. It's all becoming normal and we're being forced to keep moving our boundary line in order to accept it.'

'But what else can we do?' I asked, still sniffling. 'This is our *home*, Mike, and now Dan is part of that, but our lives and expectations are miles apart!'

'This kid doesn't want a home, love – he simply needs a base and that's what we're up against. Truth is, we're not meeting his needs and you know it's literally in our job description to meet a child's needs. So, that's what we should do from now on; if all he needs is food, a bed and a base from which to operate, then that's what we should provide.'

'But that's ridiculous!' I said, feeling myself getting worked up again. 'All kids – all humans, in fact – need interaction, love, guidance, support and someone there advocating for them.'

'Not this kid, sadly,' Mike said. 'This kid obviously gets all that from the street. To him, all we represent is somewhere to get his head down, food in his belly, and don't forget, we are a safe place, in a different part of town, and that probably helps him too.'

We continued our conversation throughout tea and then all through cleaning the dishes, and again later as we sat on the sofa with the TV playing largely to itself. Much as it went against everything I always believed in, what Mike was saying made perfect sense. It wouldn't be easy, but all we had to work with was what we had in front of us and, for our own sanity, all we could do was operate within that.

As Mike said, by now, Daniel must realise that we *did* actually care about him. He must know that nurture, love and care *were* on offer in this household, no matter what. But if he chose not to accept that, then the bare minimum he could take from us was, as Mike had already listed, a base, food, clean clothes and his pocket money. Already we had spelled out to him that we would follow the law regardless, which meant reporting him missing every single occasion he didn't come home on time and refusing to have drugs in our house. This had clearly seemed perfectly acceptable to Daniel and he didn't fear the police or repercussions at the moment, so, really, we were all on the same page.

I felt much better and clearer now about going forward, and with all that in mind, Mike and I actually enjoyed a couple of hours watching *Game of Thrones*, before having to pause the telly at half nine.

'You make a coffee,' I said, 'and I'll call the police and EDT. And don't start watching again till I'm done, love, okay?' Then glancing at the screen, I smiled wistfully. 'Oh, I'd love to own dragons, wouldn't you?'

Mike laughed and shook his head. 'You already are a mother of bloody dragons,' he said. 'Don't forget all the little buggers you've reared!'

'Charming,' I said as I picked up the phone.

'Technically,' the police officer said, after I'd explained things and given a long and detailed description of Daniel, 'he's not really missing yet, is he, Mrs Watson? I know you say he's not on the train, but he could still get home for ten; he might be in a car with a mate dropping him off.'

'He's 15!' I said. 'I can't imagine he has mates who even drive yet, let alone have cars, and anyway, he's definitely not coming home. He practically confirmed it before he left. I've told you his friend's address and the town he might be getting up to God knows what in, that his phone's off and that he's vulnerable, so please, can you at least put him on your system?'

'I'll do that,' the officer said, sighing as though this was a pointless task, 'and I'll inform my colleagues across town so that they can be on the lookout. Is there anything else?'

'No, thank you,' I said, reminding myself that I'd just agreed with Mike to simply follow the guidelines and not let it affect me. 'I'll leave it with you and get on to the out-of-hours team at social services.'

Next, I phoned EDT to let them know Dan was missing and that I'd already reported it to the police.

They noted it all on their system and told me if they got any news throughout the night, they'd let me know.

Finally, I sent another text to Mikey's mum, Carol. But since she'd not read my earlier message – according to my read receipt, anyway – I held out little hope of her responding.

So, jobs done, procedures followed and systems put in place, half an hour after starting my calls, we were sitting down again with our new favourite show. And I was really surprised that I wasn't feeling my usual gut-churning anxiety when something like this happened. Could I have finally found a way to channel Mike?

Neither of us slept very well, however. I suppose it was a step too far to expect that we'd be able to put it all to one side and then just go to bed as if everything were normal. Of course we couldn't – we were waiting for a call that we didn't really expect to come, but could have, and then we'd be up and waiting for police to bring Daniel back to us. I supposed it might be something like being a doctor on call, trying to snatch a bit of rest between emergencies: your body, primed and braced for it, won't let you.

No call came, however, not until almost exactly the time Mike's alarm started trilling. I duly snatched up my phone, mentally preparing myself for it, but the news wasn't what I'd expected.

'I'm just calling to let you know that Dan hasn't yet been located,' the officer said. 'We've just changed shifts, so I wanted to update you and ask if there was any chance he'd come home of his own volition?'

After checking his room – door still open, bed still empty – I told them Daniel hadn't been home, so the officer assured me that they were all still out looking and that I shouldn't worry too much.

'I know you will, but honestly, kids of that age, from Dan's background, they do this type of thing all the time. Though it could help if you had a recent photo that I could share with my officers.'

'I don't,' I said, but I could at least direct him to a Facebook account I'd found. 'He has a pretty recent photo on there,' I added, 'but his hair is much shorter now – not that it will matter, because he always has a hoodie on, with the hood usually pulled over his head.'

'Don't they all!' the officer said drolly, before thanking me for my help.

Mike went off to work, telling me to try and have a good day, and I decided I'd jump in the car and go and do some shopping. I needed some food items, plus some bits and bobs of make-up I'd been promising myself. Retail therapy always worked for me during testing times and since there was nothing to report to Christine yet anyway, and the police could call my mobile, there seemed little point in staying indoors.

And it proved to be helpful, this chunk of normality. A reminder that most lives were ordered and calm. Watching young mums pushing trolleys, in which sat imperious toddlers, retired couples holding hands and clutching his-n-hers baskets, youngsters hoovering up wraps, cans of pop, chocolate, grab-bags of crisps … It was like an emotional shot in the arm. And on the way home, I decided that before I called Christine, I would once again try and make contact with Mikey's mum, Carol – she might have heard something from her son, after all.

I called her mobile four times before she answered, though she didn't say why she took so long. Or why she'd not responded to my messages of the previous day.

So I started with that: 'I was hoping to speak to you yesterday—'

'I know,' she huffed back. 'Some of us have to go to *work*.'

I was stung, but there was no point in responding to that. Instead I just told her that Daniel was missing and asked her if Mikey was home.

'No, he isn't,' she snapped. 'He's not been home all night. Wait till the little bastard does get here, I'm gonna kill him!'

Not helpful at all, and her tone was very different to when I'd last spoken to her. It didn't take a rocket scientist to see where she was coming from. To her mind, I'm sure, this was all down to Daniel, even if she stopped short of saying so.

Having promised I'd let her know if I heard anything, and she likewise, I called Christine and explained everything to her too.

She was very sympathetic, but, like Mike, also very pragmatic.

'Look, Casey,' she said, 'you need to step back and get on with your day. There's nothing you can do but wait, so just do that. The police will be in touch when they find him, and tough as I know it is, just leave them to it. You'll have enough to deal with when they eventually bring him home.'

You mean back to his base, I silently corrected her, and in all probability, it will happen again, just as soon as he has slept it off and had his food and a change of clothes. What did strike me though was that she was wrong about one thing. She'd said, 'tough as I know it is' and, historically, she'd been right, because leaving it to the police was something I usually found extremely hard to do when a child in my care went AWOL. Often, I'd be in my car, scouring the streets anyway. This time, however, leaving it to the police had proved easy.

A good thing? Perhaps. But also telling.

Chapter 15

This is awful to admit, but, shockingly, two more days passed before we saw Daniel again, and for that two days, it felt as if a weight had been lifted from my shoulders. And on day two, when Christine phoned me for an update, I felt duty-bound to be honest with her and admit how I felt, plus qualifying it with just how guilty that made me feel.

'Oh, don't feel guilty, Casey,' she said. 'It's perfectly understandable. He's put you right through the wringer, that boy. I hope you're both coping, lovey, and I hope you haven't been living on nothing but coffee, either. I know what you're like!'

It was a welcome moment of levity and I duly couldn't help but laugh. 'You do indeed,' I said, 'but, no, I know it's taken me a while to get there, but I'm following Mike's lead now and taking an "it is what it is" attitude. Though trust me, when he returns, I shall be needing something a bit stronger than coffee. *If* he does, that is …'

Christine chuckled. And it was almost at exactly that moment when I saw something move out of the corner of my eye. I turned slightly. I was right. Because out of the snug window, I could see that a police car had pulled up outside.

'Good lord,' I said. 'Chris, I'm going to have to go. The police are here, so I imagine they must have found him. I'll call you back when I know what's going on.'

I ran to the door and opened it to find a police officer standing on my front step with Daniel at his side. I took in the state of him as the officer introduced himself. Although he had his hood up and head bowed, I could tell by his stance that he felt defeated. He was clutching a large pizza box under his arm and looked to be almost propping himself up on the side of the house.

'Come on in,' I said, quickly glancing up and down the street to see who might be watching. Unfortunately, my neighbours would have been well used to seeing police cars at our house over the time we'd lived there, but thankfully, almost all of them knew what we did for a living. 'We'll go through to the kitchen and then you can tell me where the hell you've been for the last two nights.' I directed this at Daniel and as he glanced up at me, I noticed he had bruising on his cheek and a black eye. 'What's happened to you?' I asked him as I sat down opposite the officer. 'And sit down, you need to be part of this.'

Daniel shook his head. 'No, I don't, so I'm not,' he said flatly. 'I want to go to sleep and I'm not saying fuck-all anyways, so …'

I was fuming but fought to keep control. 'Go ahead, then,' I said, 'for now, at least. But I'm telling you, mister, you *will* listen to what I have to say, when I'm ready, and you *will* be answering my questions. You got that?'

Something about my tone or demeanour must have deterred Daniel from answering back in his usual manner. He simply nodded and then went off upstairs.

'He's been arrested for possession of cannabis and an unknown substance which we are having tested,' the officer explained, after Daniel had gone. 'And he's bailed to your address now until his hearing, but he will need a solicitor and has been given a card from the duty officer. So, if you can make sure he rings them, and his social worker,' he added, 'once the summons comes through.'

'So, he was actually charged?' I asked, 'and not just arrested and questioned?'

''Fraid so,' the officer confirmed. 'He was found with the stuff on him. Like I said, definite for the cannabis, and the other stuff we believe is cocaine, but we're having that tested for clarity. There's a lot of other stuff going around at the minute – crushed pills, ketamine … they all look very similar.'

'Great,' I said sadly. 'Now he'll definitely have a record. Brilliant start for someone who could potentially be job seeking in the near future.'

The police officer was looking at me with a kind, but very jaded, expression. 'You never know, love, in some cases something like this is all it takes – a charge, a night in the cells and a court appearance – it scares some of them half to death and they turn it round. Fingers crossed this is the case here, eh?'

'Where did you find him?' I asked. 'Where has he been for the last two nights?'

'Not sure if he's been there the whole time, but he was found sleeping on the floor of a known drug dealer. That guy is now in custody for various charges, including county lines drug dealing and using minors to do this. He won't be out for a while, but I have to warn you it's a big family network, so he won't be the last who's exploiting these young ones.'

'And the state of him? The bruises and black eye, any idea how that came about?'

The officer chuckled and stood up to leave. 'No idea at all,' he said. 'We did ask, a few times, but the silly sod just kept saying "no comment" – refused to say another word apart from those two. I'd say he's either been watching too many cop shows and thinks that's the get-out-of-jail-free card, or one of his friends has told him that's the cool thing to say to any questions a police officer might ask.'

Silly sod indeed, I thought, as I stood up as well. There was nothing remotely cool about the line that had been crossed now. 'And what about his friend?' I asked. 'Did you find him as well?'

'Friend?'

'His friend Mikey.'

The officer shook his head. 'I don't know anything about another lad, sorry. He was on his own and, as I say, he's not saying anything. Perhaps he'll tell you when he's slept it off. Anyway, I'd better get on …'

'Yes,' I said, showing him out. 'Sorry. Of course.'

So perhaps, I thought, Mikey wasn't even involved. Which had to be good, didn't it? Or was it? Had Daniel simply moved on to bigger, badder friends?

After the police officer left, I phoned Christine straight back to let her know Daniel was back with us, but sleeping, and I told her about the impending court appearance and what the officer had said.

'Right,' Christine said, 'don't worry about repeating it all again to Phoebe, I'll do that, but please can you fill out one of your major incident forms and email it to me and her, just so we've ticked all the boxes our end. Oh, and don't be doing all the work for the lad. Once you have a solicitor on the phone, make him speak to them. He needs to know there's a process after an arrest and he will have to be part of it.'

I left it two more hours before deciding to go and confront Daniel about his escapades and I walked into his room determined not to stand for any refusals to talk or engage. I had my mojo back and I wasn't afraid to use it.

'Time to spill the beans, kid,' I said brightly as I yanked back the curtains and opened his bedroom window. 'Come on, rise and shine, Dan! No point dragging the duvet round your neck either, because I swear to you, I don't care in the least if you're half naked. I will drag it off the bed.'

'Oh, my gorrrrd ... oh, my dayyys,' Daniel said as he swung his legs off the bed and sank his head into his heads. 'I'm so tired! Please, I beg, just let me sleep a bit. This is like torture, man.'

'I'm not a man,' I said, just as brightly as before, 'and no, until we've had this discussion, so I can finish off my notes, you can't sleep. The sooner you start talking, the sooner I'll leave you to it, and don't dare think about "no commenting" to me, I'm telling you now.'

I swear I don't know where this sudden bravado had come from, but I was definitely making the most of it.

'So, like I said, spill.'

'You're gonna just grass me up if I do,' Daniel said, looking up from his bedside, highlighting his now-vivid bruises. 'You just said you're gonna put it all in your notes.'

'Of course I am,' I said, 'I have to do that, it's part of my job, and in any case, they already know most of it, because the police file it online just as I have to. Now I need to know where you've been, what you've been doing and how did you come to be injured?'

'Oh, my days,' Daniel said again. 'I've just been round my mate's hood, chilling and that—'

'Mikey's?'

He nodded. 'We did a few pills, smoked a bit of weed and obviously we went out selling, 'cos *obvs* it costs money. Like, they give us weed and stuff for free, but then we have to pay them back by selling their gear, it's no biggie. I don't know why the cops had to bust that guy's door down just to find me, I'm gonna be in trouble for that now.'

'Well, no, you're not, Dan,' I said. 'That guy has been sent to jail for lots of other offences as well as harbouring you and your daft mate, Mikey, and the other reason is because you can't go back there. I mean, you must know that. Don't you think you're in enough trouble as it is?'

Daniel huffed at me then and stood up to look out the window. He was quiet for a minute or two, but then turned around to face me. 'I'm sorry, Casey, and I know you and Mike are trying to look after me, but I've no choice, I have to go back.'

'No, Dan, you don't, and you can't!' I insisted. 'It would be stupid to go back. And very dangerous. Look at your face for a start, black eye, bruised cheek and nose – who did that to you and what's to stop them doing it again?'

Daniel sighed, then went to sit back on his bed. 'Like I said, I don't have a choice.' He pointed to his face. 'How do you think this happened?' he asked. 'I'll tell you, and you can write it up in your little notes if you have to. Me and Mikey had been on gear all night long and the guys told us the next day that we had to work off our debt, but to make it quicker they loaned me this fuck-off electric bike thing – worth a fortune, they told me. I was only gone 10 minutes round the block when these two guys with black bandanas round their faces came running at me, knocked me off the bike and beat me up. Then they nicked off with the bike. I swear down I was scared to death of telling Long Boy – he's like the boss, and it was his bike, but he was proper cool about it, man. Just told me not to worry and that I could work it off to pay him back.'

'That's just madness!' I said. 'There's no way I can allow you to go off dealing to repay some scumbag dealer for a bloody bike that he forced you out on in the first place, no way at all!'

'Whatever,' Daniel said wearily. 'Look, I told you, right? So, can I sleep now? Look, I swear, I *am* sorry. I don't have a choice anymore though – they'll kill me if I let them down.'

Chapter 16

The police had followed up with a phone call to ask how things were going and they promised to do all they could to help me, at least as far as they could. And they obviously meant it; they told me about a service they provided which included ongoing support from a drugs liaison officer – something I was still waiting to hear about from Phoebe.

But this was apparently different. 'He's actually part of our team of PLOs,' the officer explained, 'our police liaison officers, but with a focus on working with clients who have been misusing drugs and/or alcohol.'

The officer was clearly as efficient as he'd sounded because only a couple of days later, at 11 in the morning, my mobile rang with an unknown number, which turned out to be a man called Tom Griffin, the drugs liaison officer they'd told me would be in touch with me.

He explained what his role would be, should I wish to make use of his service. Basically, he worked with all ages of people, but particularly with young adults who were deemed at risk of offending and were known to take drugs. He was part of the police force, but worked independently and tailored all of his sessions individually; he started out with a home visit or two, where he tried to gain the person's trust, and they would talk about the destructive path drugs always led to.

'Then, hopefully, once I build up some kind of relationship, we go out and about a few times, for a McDonald's or a coffee or something, and we take it from there. Ideally, I can convince your lad that he can still have an exciting and full life without resorting to such risk-taking,' he said. 'And we could start right now, if you like. You simply tell me anything you'd like me to know.'

I explained everything that had happened over the last few days, making sure I emphasised the danger I believed Daniel was in, now that some dealer had his hooks into him because of the business of the e-bike getting stolen.

'Oh, no,' Tom said. 'You're certainly right that it's a jungle out there, but the theft of the e-bike is almost certainly something the dealers would have set up themselves.'

'Set up?'

'Absolutely. The bike almost certainly wouldn't have been stolen – well, not from Dan himself, as he thinks happened. It probably would have been stolen in the first instance, obviously, but by the dealers themselves.

Who'd have then lent it to Dan, from whom it got nicked, but it will actually just have been choreographed to *look* like a robbery, but have all been arranged prior. A set-up. They'll have paid someone to beat him up and steal the bike from him, but it will have gone straight back to them. This is how they keep the kids in line. They've then got to keep working to pay off the cost of the bike that was "stolen" while in their possession – it's how they keep them in their debt.'

'But if it's so common, why don't these kids know that's what's happening?'

'Oh, I imagine some do. But how do they go about proving it? It's dog eat dog, isn't it? And the dog with the biggest cojones is always going to be the one who holds the power.'

It was all so depressing, and made even more so by the simplicity of the set-up. Not to mention the sheer callous evil of it all.

'The police and social services have mentioned county lines a few times,' I said. 'I'm not exactly clear on what that is, apart from that it's to do with drugs, but do you think this is what Dan is involved with?' I asked.

'Quite possibly,' Tom said, 'although until further arrests are made, we can't be sure, but yes, this is an ongoing operation with this particular gang that Dan has hooked up with. And to answer your question, briefly, county lines is the name we give to an organised criminal gang who recruit, groom or entice usually vulnerable kids into dealing their drugs for them in more rural areas. Hence the electric bikes etc. as this gives them more scope to get out of the area. Anyway, these kids quickly find themselves in debt to the dealers and are almost always terrified of them, either due to a beating, or hearing about brutal beatings from others, and that's it in a nutshell.'

'Oh my God,' I said. 'And that sounds just like what Dan has been explaining to me, but he just won't listen to anything I say. Please, I'd love to take you up on your offer to help, and the sooner the better. Social services have offered a drugs counsellor, but I'm not sure now if that will be helpful – not as helpful as you could be anyway, as you're at the sharp end of this county lines thing. Besides, it could be weeks before they get the go-ahead to set something up.'

'Ah, all the red tape and the budgets,' Tom said knowingly. 'Annoying as hell when you need something yesterday, but yes, I'm happy to help. Let me look in my diary when I get back to the office and I'll call you with a few dates and times I have free. Don't worry, it will be in the next few days. I'm not governed by the same tight budgets thankfully.'

I felt encouraged by my conversation with Tom, and not just about the possibility of him helping us, but because we could now spell out to Daniel what had *really* been going on. Which would surely open his eyes a little, wouldn't it? But I also knew from the experience of all our previous conversations that he simply wasn't listening to anything we had to say. So it proved after he finally surfaced around six that evening in search of food and we sat him down and tried to get him to see what was happening.

'So?' he said. 'Even if it is true, it doesn't change anything, does it?'

'You say that,' Mike said, 'but things *can* be changed. Son, you know the score. The best way to keep you safe, now all this has been happening, is for us to speak to Phoebe and see about getting you moved on to somewhere away from here. Somewhere far away, it will have to be – right away from everyone you know, lad. Somewhere these people can't find you.'

I was shocked. Although we were both getting to the point of admitting defeat, this was the first time it had been laid bare to Daniel as a next step. We'd not even discussed our thoughts with one another yet, let alone with Christine. But perhaps Mike was trying to jolt Daniel into understanding the seriousness of the road he was on. If so, it clearly wasn't hitting the spot. Indeed, Daniel's expression was little short of withering.

'You think?' he said contemptuously. 'You really have *no* idea, do you?'

I could see Mike making the mental effort to ignore Daniel's tone. 'I reckon I have more of an idea than you think, lad,' he said evenly. 'Us, the people around us – all the people who are trying *their level best* to help you get on a better path, to keep you *safe* – we didn't come down in the last shower of rain. And the way things are headed here … well, I don't see there's any alternative.

Breaking Point

If we can't keep you away from these people – who are exploiting you, son, you *have* to see that – then what else *can* be done? If you think social services are just going to stand by and watch you getting deeper and deeper into drugs and criminality, then you're very much mistaken. You can believe it or not, your choice, but we do all care, and very much, about what happens to you.'

'Yeah, right.' Daniel's expression was even more withering. And not without reason. His time in care might have seen him with a roof over his head, but the caring bit … well, didn't he have every right to feel cynical? I thought back to our Tyler. If only, I thought sadly, we'd encountered Daniel earlier. But that was pointless thinking.

'Anyway,' Daniel went on before either of us could formulate a response to that, 'so they move me somewhere else. What difference? Because I'll run away, I'll just run straight back again. Doesn't matter where they send me, where I end up. I'll find my way back.' He sighed heavily. 'And if youse two won't have me, I'll find another place to go. No disrespect, like,' he said, his gaze moving between the two of us, calm, assessing, 'but it's *you* that doesn't get it. Like I already told you, if I don't work to pay that bill off, they'll find me and they'll kill me.'

* * *

'Well,' said Mike, once Daniel had gone back up to his room. 'That's certainly given us plenty to chew on.'

I shook my head wearily. 'And just what are we supposed to do now? You know, I really thought – really hoped – that spelling out to him how cleverly he's being played, being manipulated, might just jolt him into seeing things differently. I mean, he's obviously terrified of these criminals. That's a given, that's exactly where they want these kids. But why can't he see that he can be helped to escape their clutches?'

'Because it's not his world, Case. Officialdom, the law, social services … I doubt he has an ounce of trust in any of them. And why would he? He's been operating in a world where they count for next to nothing.'

'Except his father went to prison. That must surely count for something? Went to prison and left him without a home.'

'I don't think that matters. The law he respects – crazy though it seems to us – is the law of the streets, the famous "jungle". He even said so himself.'

I ploughed my hands through my hair. This was hopeless. It was like Daniel was running in a race to the bottom and we were trying desperately to catch him up and stop him. Trouble was, it felt like he was already three laps ahead. Could we catch him now? I genuinely didn't think so.

* * *

Breaking Point

The whole situation with Daniel having become so entrenched, and so worrying, I couldn't concentrate on the movie Mike had chosen to distract us – a gentle heart-warming Brit-flick – so when my mobile phone went, at a little after 9 p.m., it was almost as if I had willed it to ring. Even though any call at that time was generally not good news, any distraction from the intended distraction was welcome.

It was one call, however, that I definitely had not expected – one from EDT. I stared as the number flashed on my screen. Yes, I got calls from EDT from time to time, nothing unusual about that, but for a moment or two I did a mental double take. Daniel was upstairs in his bedroom, wasn't he? Or was he? Because, of course, I assumed it must be about him. But no, that was ridiculous – I'd passed his bedroom and heard him in there only half an hour ago.

Mike and I exchanged a puzzled look and I put the call to speaker while he paused the movie.

'I am *so* sorry to trouble you at this time,' the duty officer started, 'but we're in a bind and I really hope you can help. And before I go on,' he added, just as I was about to interrupt him, 'we do know that you have a particularly challenging teenager in currently, so obviously we wouldn't be asking you if there was anyone else who could take this. And we have tried, I promise.'

He went on to explain that they had a six-year-old girl needing a bed for the night. 'And just the one night, if it's all you can manage, Mrs Watson. But ideally the whole weekend, if possible. She literally has nowhere to go right now. Is there any way at all that you could take her?'

This was certainly a turn-up. The Emergency Duty Team were an out-of-hours service that ran nationally. They were made up of a team of social workers that worked day jobs, but also had to be on a rota to be on call, and to answer phone calls throughout the night, every night, from members of the public who had welfare concerns, or from foster carers who needed help. But I knew, from my recent conversations with Christine, that they were really struggling to recruit enough people to keep the rotas filled. Mike shrugged, in his now-familiar 'it is what it is' kind of way.

'Where is she now?' I asked.

'In the care of the police, and in only the clothes she was stood up in. We don't yet have all the details but she was found a couple of hours ago, apparently by a neighbour who was out walking her dog. She was literally wandering the streets. And when the neighbour took her back home, it was to find that the front door was open and the girl's mother – who she obviously lives with – wasn't there. And right now, it looks like there's no other family to call on. I mean, there might be, and we're working on it, but right now, that isn't an option – and it seems the neighbour doesn't reckon we're likely to find anyone, either. So, for now, that's how things stand. We just need a safe space for her to stay, at least overnight, and hope for some clarity in the morning.'

Much as I was reticent – it was late, and who knew what kind of state the child would be in? – there was no arguing that we did have a bed for her. And with Daniel likely not to surface again until tomorrow afternoon, we could, at least in theory, provide that. They clearly were in a bind, or they wouldn't have called us, and the thought of the poor child having to spend the night in a police station obviously tugged at my heartstrings. Mike's too. I could tell by his expression. But I still needed to make the situation clear, because I knew all too well how these things often went.

'I think we can manage over this weekend,' I told the man, 'but Daniel really is proving to be very difficult to manage, and he's also very volatile, so it will almost certainly be better for her if you could find somewhere calmer if it turns out that she needs to be in care any longer than that.'

'Thank you *so* much,' the man said, his tone noticeably more relaxed now. 'And of course, that's a given. And we'll obviously stay in touch. There's no one been assigned the child yet, but if we have any further information, we'll of course be in touch over the weekend. Her name is Molly, by the way.'

So that was it: film now on hold for the forseeable. With a little one whose arrival was going to be soon to pretty imminent, my next job would be to dash up the stairs and make up said bed.

'It never rains, eh?' Mike said ruefully. He nodded towards the ceiling. 'So let's hope the volcano upstairs remains dormant.'

Chapter 17

Molly looked like the proverbial rabbit caught in headlights. A tiny little thing – she looked nearer four than six – she had wide-set blue eyes, currently trained fixedly on my own, and blonde hair, straggling down almost to her waist. Dirty blonde hair, to be more accurate, both in colour and in state. In fact, even in just the light that spilled out from our hallway, I could see she had that patina of long-ingrained dirt on her skin that you'd normally expect to see on someone who'd been living on the streets for a very long time. What kind of hellhole had she come from that she could be in such a state? I felt immediately glad that we'd agreed to take her in.

I ushered them both inside and settled the acquiescent but silent child down on the sofa, where she immediately picked up one of the comics I'd thought to bring down and a biscuit from the plate I'd put beside her. It was only around 20 minutes since I'd had the call from EDT and I could tell by the expression on the on-call social worker's face that he was up to his eyes and keen to be on his way. He looked close to retirement age and had heavy bags under his eyes. I immediately felt sorry for him, knowing that this might not be the only call-out he had to make tonight, and that he would be on shift right through until 9 a.m., when the day team clocked in. But, that's how the Emergency Duty Team worked. There would be one social worker covering the phones, on hand all night to give advice to any foster carers or members of the public that needed it, and then another one, like this guy, who worked from home, but had to be on hand all through the night to pick up or drop off any emergency placements.

We stepped away a little, across to the kitchen area. 'I know it's unlikely,' I said to the man, who'd introduced himself as Robert Beck, 'but have you managed to glean any information at all that might be helpful?'

Robert shook his head and then wiped his hand across his forehead as if sweating. 'Not really,' he said, 'apart from the fact her mum is called Sophia and has still not been located. According to Molly, she had gone out to collect her medicine, but had been gone a long time, so Molly decided to go out to try and find her.' He sighed before adding, 'Other than that, nothing. Oh,' he added, watching the child devour a second biscuit, 'and all she's had to eat since the police picked her up is a bag of crisps, and she drank a glass of squash, so she's probably very hungry. Do you mind if I get going? I have a feeling I've a busy night ahead.' He looked up at the sky then, through our window, and pointed. 'Full moon,' he said as if the grey ball in the sky were entirely responsible for his plight. 'Always the same.'

I watched in amusement as Mike walked the man back towards the hall and then turned my attention to the little girl, who was now staring intently at me. Though it was late, it seemed unthinkable to put the poor mite straight to bed in the state she was in. Plus, a full belly and a nice warm bath might help her sleep better.

'Are you hungry, sweetie?' I asked her, while Mike saw Robert off. 'Come on, let's go into the kitchen and I'll make you something proper to eat.'

She nodded shyly, then got up and followed me across to the breakfast bar, where she immediately clambered up onto one of the bar stools.

'How about a sandwich?' I suggested, reaching to grab bread from the bread bin. But her eyes had obviously alighted on something else.

'I like pizza,' she said, pointing towards a spot just beyond the open door to the utility room, where there was a big box for all our paper and cardboard recycling. Out of it was poking a greasy takeaway pizza box – the one Daniel had arrived home with that morning and, typically, forcibly wedged into the fridge. I'd since hoicked it out and relocated the remaining slices into a plastic storage box. To give them to Molly felt like a wilfully inflammatory act, but I was feeling mutinous. Besides, if he was that desperate to eat pizza when he finally emerged tomorrow, I could always dial in another.

'We have pizza,' I confirmed, smiling. 'I'll warm some up for you, shall I?'

But Molly shook her head. 'I like it cold,' she said.

'Really?'

Again, the shy nod. Evidence, perhaps, that this was how she was normally served it? When she was fed anything, that was. Because she wolfed down two of the four enormous remaining slices – it was one of those stuffed-crust XXXL takeaway pizzas that seemed to be the norm now – and in such a rapacious manner that even Mike, who could put away pizza with the best of them, felt moved to comment.

'You were certainly hungry, then!' he observed brightly as she licked tomato-ey goo from her fingers. We exchanged a glance – she'd obviously not been fed properly in days.

Molly giggled and then burped. 'Oopsie,' she said, 'that was a big one, wasn't it?'

'That certainly was,' Mike said, laughing. 'Now I bet you would love to go upstairs with Casey and have a lovely, bubbly bath with all the smellies, wouldn't you?'

Molly wrinkled her nose: 'Not smelly,' she said. 'We can put shampoo in it, make it nice.'

'Great idea,' I said, reaching for her hand. 'Come on then, let's go, but we need to be a bit quiet so we don't wake anybody else up, okay?'

Breaking Point

Thankfully, Molly just nodded and didn't question who that 'anybody' might be; we could deal with that introduction tomorrow. In the meantime, now that she'd been fed, I needed to get this child cleaned up and into bed. The poor kid seemed half-starved, the way she'd wolfed that pizza down.

It was an assumption that seemed even more starkly confirmed once I'd taken her upstairs and run a bath. She was stick-thin, her ribs like a washboard on her torso and, as I'd first noticed, her skin was ingrained with dirt. And not the kind of dirt seen on a child who's been making mud pies in the garden. It was dirt that had settled and become absorbed into her pores, and had taken up residence beneath fingernails and toenails. How had this child remained under the radar?

A long time ago – perhaps as long as two decades – we'd taken in two young siblings in similarly wretched circumstances. They had been both sexually abused and hideously neglected to the extent that the dirt between their toes was bedded in so completely that it almost looked like they had webbed feet. It had been so painful for them, and a truly horrific task to perform. We'd had to remove it really carefully, in dark waxy plugs which smelt almost indescribable, and had also left livid red skin in their place. Thankfully, this wasn't that bad, but it was still hard to look at – how could a child be treated so despicably? Except, grim as it looked, the reality was that this was almost certainly the child of a mother who (and I'd bet my last quid on it) was probably incapable of looking after herself, let alone her daughter.

I kept up a soft stream of chatter to Molly as I bathed her. She was quiet, acquiescent, not at all fazed by my bathing her, which was a bit of a worry in itself. Did this child have any agency whatsoever? I'd given her my box of bath toys to play with while I did so and she'd made a beeline for a brace of battered Barbies, both naked, having long since been stripped of their clothing and sporting shocks of tatty blonde hair. So, I talked about how lovely Molly's hair was. Or would be, once I'd given it my 'magic princess hair' treatment, slathering on copious amounts of conditioner to try and disentangle clumps of hair that were fast becoming dreadlocks. There was only so much I could do, but it would at least be a start, especially if I didn't rinse it all out.

'How does that feel?' I asked her, once I'd made a decent amount of progress. Now her face was cleaner, I could see just how deathly pale and undernourished she looked.

'Nice,' she said, still busy washing her Barbies. Then, turning to look up at me, added, 'Are you an auntie?'

'Kind of,' I said. 'I'm here to take care of you till it's time to take you home to your mummy.'

'Before bedtime?' She looked shocked at this.

'No, not before bedtime. You're going to sleep here tonight and tomorrow night too, perhaps, and—'

'Could I stay here instead?' she asked. 'And could Mummy come as well?' A pause, then, as she seemed to be thinking through her circumstances. 'And you could give her her medicine?'

It was difficult to know how to answer that. 'We don't have any of Mummy's medicine,' I eventually plumped for. 'But don't worry, sweetie. There are people who are helping Mummy, just like I am with you. Now then, how about we get you dried off and go and choose some pyjamas? I have flowery ones. And princess ones, and – I know, do you like Bluey? I have Bluey ones too.'

Which seemed to distract her – she did indeed like Bluey the TV puppy – and with the same acquiescence she'd been showing since her arrival, she allowed me to dry her off and help her into her pyjamas. Once tucked up in bed, with me perched beside her reading a story, she was asleep in a matter of minutes.

'I wonder how soon she'll reappear?' Mike pondered once I'd joined him downstairs and told him what Molly had said about her mummy's 'medicine'. 'Or where they'll find her if she doesn't,' he added, shaking his head. 'No prizes for guessing, eh?' he finished wryly. 'Because I doubt it's the kind of medicine you get on prescription.'

I took the coffee he handed me and blew on it before sipping. 'I'd say that's an absolute given, love. Which means that poor little girl is unlikely to be heading home any time soon, is she?'

A muffled thump from above made us both look towards the ceiling, but without much concern as we'd heard it so often – Daniel's game controller falling off his bed.

Mike sighed. 'And then there were two,' he observed. 'I wonder what fresh delights tomorrow has in store for us?'

The world seemed a bleak place that night.

Chapter 18

I woke late the following morning, after another fitful night's sleep, and the first thing I became aware of was the sound of someone knocking tentatively on the bedroom door. It came back to me in a rush, then – we'd taken in that little girl last night, hadn't we? So preoccupied had I been with the whole Daniel situation that the events of the previous evening had still not percolated back into my consciousness.

Mike wasn't in the bed and a mug of coffee was cooling beside me. He'd obviously thought better of waking me. In fact, I noticed, as I glanced out of the window while putting on my dressing gown, he was down in the garden, pottering among the last of his dahlias, bless him. And with that barely mentioned but definite limp. *If there's a god*, I thought, *please can you arrange for that knee op appointment to come through?* To have that imminently would take matters out of our hands. Which would make everything feel so much less fraught.

Having grabbed the lukewarm coffee, I went across and opened the bedroom door, causing Molly, who was sitting cross-legged on the landing clutching one of the bath-time Barbies, to leap, startled, to her feet. I wondered how long she'd been out there. 'It's okay, sweetheart,' I reassured her, as she clutched the doll to her chest. 'Goodness me, what a sleepyhead I've been. You must have been wondering where I was! Have you been up for long?'

She shook her head. She'd got some colour back in her cheeks, I was pleased to see, but, as with last night, she still displayed a strange lack of anxiety about her situation. She seemed more bemused, really, but with an acceptance of what was happening to her that worried me. She was in a strange house, with strangers, in another child's pyjamas, yet her demeanour suggested that being plucked from the street and brought to us late at night was no different from having a sleepover with a relative. What kind of life had she been living? Depressingly, I could picture it all too well.

Glancing over only briefly at the closed door of Daniel's bedroom, I quickly ushered her downstairs. 'I'll bet you're hungry,' I said, as I followed her down. 'What sort of things do you like for breakfast?'

'Do you have jam?' she asked. 'I like jam.'

'On toast?'

I saw her head shake. 'I just like it with a spoon.'

A picture leapt at me – of her sitting cross-legged on the floor, scooping up spoonfuls from a jar in her lap.

Breaking Point

Then another, of a child often left to her own devices, and, too small and/or young to use kitchen equipment, foraging for things to eat as best she could.

'Well …' I said, pushing further speculation from my mind. We'd find out Molly's backstory soon enough. 'I think it's even nicer on toast. With lots of butter. I have strawberry and raspberry, and, if we're lucky, there might even be a little apricot left. Do you have a favourite?' I went on as we went through into the kitchen-diner.

She turned and shrugged, lifting her skinny arms and shoulders. 'Just jam flavoured, really.'

Mike walked in through the back door just as we arrived in the kitchen and, as with most of the kids since we'd moved into the house, Molly made a beeline once again for one of the bar stools.

'Well, good morning, young lady,' Mike said brightly. Then he clapped his hands together. 'Perfect timing as well. Now then, who's up for a bacon sarnie?'

'Not me and Molly,' I said, 'we're having some lovely jam on hot toast, aren't we, Molly?'

She smiled sweetly. 'If that man's having some bacon, I'll have some too,' she said, glancing shyly at Mike, 'and my jam too, I like jam.'

I laughed. 'Well, I think we can manage that,' I said before pointing towards Mike, 'and that man is called Mike, and I'm called Casey, but it's okay if you forget. You can just ask me to remember for you, okay?'

Molly was just delightful, a really refreshing respite from the challenging times we'd been having, and we spent the morning watching silly TV shows, colouring in and dressing up the old, battered Barbies she'd asked if she could have from upstairs. I got the strong sense that having such toys was a real luxury. Which made me sad, because you could pick up toys for next to nothing in the charity shops – all you needed was to make that small effort – and that she seemed not to have had many hinted at the darkness of her home life.

As we'd expected, Daniel didn't surface until mid-afternoon, his eventual appearance having been heralded half an hour earlier, first by the thudding of the rap music starting up, then the sound of the shower, at which point I told Molly that the source of the noise was a lad called Daniel, who was also staying with us.

She took this in without comment – just a nod of acknowledgement. Though when he appeared in the kitchen – in trackies and T-shirt, heavy hoodie and his usual grubby trainers – I saw a flicker of anxiety in her eyes.

With Molly on the sofa, it was a while before Daniel spotted her and when he did, to our surprise, he just responded with 'Alright?' and raised a quick hand in greeting, as if it was no surprise to him to see her there; almost as if they were already acquainted. Which, of course, they weren't. Not unless they'd met on the landing in the small hours, which I felt pretty sure wasn't the case. But then I supposed it did make sense. If your home is a children's home, you see kids coming and going all the time. Ditto staff members, sadly.

Breaking Point

'This is Molly. She's staying for the weekend,' I told him as he opened the fridge and peered into its depths, presumably after his pizza. I tensed for a moment, bracing myself for the inevitable inquisition. But then he seemed to change his mind. Perhaps he assumed he must have eaten it, or mislaid it on the journey home. In any event, he shut the fridge door and went to pour himself a glass of water, which he glugged down, a full pint of it, before replying.

'Safe,' he said. 'Yo, Molly,' and raised is hand a second time. Then, turning back, 'I'm heading off to Mikey's, by the way. So, I'm going to need some money for the train fare.'

Mike pulled his wallet from his back pocket and pulled out a 10-pound note.

Despite the conversations we'd already had about how much pocket money he was allowed weekly, Daniel took it from him with a look of surprise and annoyance. Was he seriously expecting that we'd give him more? 'A tenner?' he growled. 'Is that it? That's well tight!' he huffed. 'A tenner don't last two fucking minutes these days.'

'Ten pounds is a lot more than some kids your age get,' Mike pointed out. 'And we've been given our orders so that's that. And, by the way, you know the rules. That's enough of that language, lad, okay?'

There was a moment when Daniel's body language looked decidedly pugilistic but he seemed to think better of taking Mike on. Instead, he stomped back into the hall, now swearing even louder, and before either of us had had a chance to remind him of his coming home time, had turned the latch and pulled open the front door. Which he then slammed with such wall-rattling force behind him that it caused Molly, who'd barely taken her eyes off him since he'd come into the kitchen, to jolt in shock and then burst into tears.

I rushed to comfort her, sitting beside her and scooping her into my embrace, aware as I did so that Mike was considering going after him. I could see the anger in his eyes and noticed the way his hands were bunched into fists.

'Leave it, love,' I mouthed at him. 'Just let him go.'

The same man from EDT – Robert Beck – called half an hour later, so while Mike kept Molly entertained by helping her with a jigsaw puzzle, I went off into the snug to hear what he had to say.

The news wasn't good, but it wasn't surprising either. 'The child's mother has been located,' he explained. 'Found in a local drug den that was well known to the police.'

'Oh God,' I said, 'what? And she thought it was okay to leave her little girl home alone while she did who knows what in some drug den? How did she react, knowing Molly had been picked up?'

'According to the police, the woman is a bit of an alley cat,' he said. 'She attacked the officers, kicking and screaming, but there were others there too. One guy –

her boyfriend, they said – was already fighting with her when the police turned up.'

This perhaps explained Molly's hysteria when Daniel had come down and started throwing his weight around. How many times in her young life had she witnessed male violence and aggression?

'So, what's happening now?' I asked.

'Well, she's been arrested, apparently, and charged with neglect. Seems the child had been left on her own in the house for some 36 hours and an emergency care order has also been granted, so the child's now in the care of the local authority.'

All of this was said to me in a matter-of-fact manner, making me feel as though to this guy, it was just another day at the office, which, I suppose it was.

'So, she won't be heading home any time soon then?' I said.

'Correct. So, can you definitely keep her till Monday?'

'Yes, of course. But you know our situation here, don't you?'

'Oh yes, absolutely. We're fully informed about the circumstances and know she needs to be placed elsewhere so don't worry. Someone will be in touch first thing Monday about getting her moved on.'

I hung up and remained seated in the snug. I could hear Mike laughing and Molly yelling with delight about something, and I couldn't help but wish that she were our main placement. I decided I'd stay where I was for a few more minutes and picked the phone back up. I'd ring Riley for a chat; it had been a few days and my daughter could always make me feel better. I told her all about Molly and her situation, and then about how Daniel had just been with us.

'Oh, Mum, that's awful,' Riley said. 'I mean all of it, that poor baby, and also what you and Dad are going through with Dan. Tell you what, I have loads of dolls and dress-up clothes etc. here, I'll drop some off for you. I've seen the state of those flipping Barbies you're on about – it's a wonder they don't give the poor girl nightmares!'

I laughed, 'Hey, cheeky! She loves those dolls, even though they're naked and have haircuts that would put Sweeney Todd to shame, but thanks, you've cheered me up a bit.'

'Seriously though, Mum, I know how things are. Can't you just end it with him and keep the little girl?'

Obviously, I didn't tell her that she'd just read my mind – I felt bad enough thinking it as it was. I hung up and went back to the main room to join Mike and Molly, but was surprised to see they weren't there. A loud giggle told me they were out in the garden, so I went to the back door to see what they were up to.

'Someone looks like they're having fun,' I said as I watched Mike pile pine cones into a bucket that Molly was holding.

'We're having a nature hunt,' Mike explained, 'collecting things that we can make some autumn decorations with, so that Molly can take them back home with her.'

I winced as I remembered that Molly wouldn't in fact be going home, but almost certainly to another foster carer's house. I watched her for a moment, scrambling around in the leggings and old jumper I'd managed to find in the clothes cupboard I kept specifically for foster children.

'I'll just get her a coat and hat,' I said, remembering I'd seen those as I'd been searching through earlier. Then, having ensured she was warm enough, I went back inside to make a coffee, just in time to hear my mobile phone ringing. It was Christine and she already knew all about the situation with Molly.

'It's not her though that I'm phoning about,' she said. 'Do you remember Bella? The girl you had just before Dan?'

I told her that of course I did and asked if there was a problem because I definitely wasn't in a position to take in a third child.

'No, no,' Christine went on. 'Heavens, as if! I've just had a very interesting chat with her social worker, that's all, and I thought you should know about it.'

Christine explained that the whole time Daniel had been with us, he and Bella had kept in touch via their phones. Apparently, Bella really liked Daniel, or 'Deejay' as she called him, and thought that he felt the same. The social worker had actually told Christine that Bella believed they were in a girlfriend/boyfriend relationship and that Daniel had led her to believe that this was so. However, it seemed he had had other motivations: he had used the fact that Bella was besotted with him to get her to send him money.

'What?!' I asked. 'When was this? Money to his bank?'

'All the time,' Christine confirmed. 'And yes, to his bank. I've seen the text messages where he's swearing his love to her, then asking her to send 10 or sometimes 20 pounds to his bank so that he can travel to get to see her. Of course he never did, he just wanted the money, but Bella fell for it time and time again, believing his excuses that he'd been locked up at a police station, or that you'd prevented him from leaving, or some other bull. Anyway, it all came to light when Bella's foster carer realised that the girl had gone through almost 100 pounds from her savings account. She told them everything, and, well, the carer asked me to let you know.'

I was astounded at the levels Daniel had been stooping to. Poor Bella must be in a right state, I thought. I managed to pass all of this on to Mike throughout the day and I also managed to hide my feelings from Molly as we went about business as usual at home. She was getting really tired by about 5.30, but I didn't want her to sleep or nap yet, so I got her to help me make tea – sausages and mash with peas, which she professed her love for as soon as I suggested it.

And, as I was beginning to realise was her way, she did. She ate every scrap, and all but licked the plate.

Breaking Point

With Molly having taken herself off to bed straight after tea, we were left alone in the house with our thoughts. Which were, predictably, all about Daniel. 'This is just awful,' I said to Mike, once we'd settled in our little snug and put the fire on. He was scrolling up and down the television screen, looking for something to distract us. Right now, I couldn't countenance watching any more of *Game of Thrones*. I had had quite enough of power struggles and confrontation for one day.

'It is, love,' Mike agreed. 'You know, *Jesus*, if that lad was mine ...' He let the comment hang. We both knew what he meant; we both also knew that if that lad *had* been his, he would not be the lad we were currently trying to care for. A lad that, I think we were both fast coming to understand, was incapable of accepting that care; incapable of seeing us as anything other than adversaries – problems to be dealt with. How on earth were we to ever get through to him? The claws of those wretched drug dealers were already in too deep. And the business with Bella only strengthened my conviction that this boy was beyond help, at least *our* help.

'Do you think that's what will happen?' I asked him. 'What you said to Dan on Friday about them finding a new home for him, well out of the area?'

He sighed. 'I have no idea. If we tell them the placement's over, I can't think what else they'll do. They're not going to find anyone else around here to take him on, are they? So, it's either that, or straight back to one of the local homes again. Assuming any even have any space for him.' He shook his head. 'I don't know, love. I really don't know. But that's what I'd do. Get him out. Right away. Whatever his baloney about finding his way back again. What's the alternative? They just give up on him?'

And were we too now giving up on him? Was that what Mike was thinking? Giving up on him officially? Despite us having always been clear with Christine that if we needed to, we could, the reality of doing so was another matter altogether. It was a horrible thing to contemplate.

'So, do you think we've reached the end of the road with him?'

'I'm feeling close to that, yes, love. Your shout, though. I'll support you in whatever you want to do, you know that. But what's going to change? He knows full well we can't stop him doing anything, and with this debt to those dealers …' he didn't need to spell out the implications for us '… the only change I can see on the horizon is that he ends up in custody. He's 15, remember? Only a matter of time before he gets himself nicked. And what can we do to stop that happening? Nothing. Where's he now? What's he up to?' He spread his hands in exasperation. 'I've got to be honest, love, I'm feeling claustrophobic.'

'Claustrophobic?'

'Yeah, like, I know that in theory we aren't trapped in the house, we can go out any time we like, but I do feel trapped. It's like Groundhog Day for us and we can't do anything about it. We can't even really have the grandkids around to play with Molly, even if we wanted to, for fear of what they might see or hear – it's just crap.'

The question of what Daniel might have been up to was at least partly answered a couple of hours later when there was a screeching sound outside and, a second or so later, the rhythmic thump of loud music playing. Rap, as always.

'What the hell?' said Mike, standing up and pulling the curtain aside. 'There's a car out there.' He let the curtain drop and headed out into the hall.

I got up and followed him, and when he opened the front door the music was even louder. Loud enough to wake half the street. It was a big car. A black one. An expensive-looking one – 'It's a BMW,' Mike provided – out of the back of which Daniel was now emerging. Or, rather, stumbling out, laughing. He looked either drunk or stoned, or high – possibly all three.

The car door slammed shut again and it was impossible to see who else was in there in any case, since the windows appeared to be tinted. We could only see Daniel, who was slapping his hand on the car roof, an idiotic smile on his face.

'Cheers, my boys!' he slurred. 'Catch you all tomorrow, yeah?'

The enormous car immediately screeched off again.

Daniel weaved his unsteady way up the path, grinning when he saw us, then held his hands up as he approached the front door, as if expecting us to part for him, like the sea did for Moses. 'I'm home early,' he announced as we looked at him, stoney-faced. 'So I don't need no fucking inquisition, just my pit, yeah?'

I could feel my body stiffening. Oh, he didn't need one, did he? Well, tough, because he'd certainly be getting one. But then I felt Mike's hand in mine, with which he tugged me towards him, leaving Daniel to slip past us and walk unsteadily up the stairs.

'Not now, love,' he whispered, as Daniel pinballed his way to the top before disappearing from sight on the landing. 'Let's let him sleep it off first and we'll deal with it in the morning. And when I say deal with it, I mean *deal* with it. I'm done, we're not putting up with any more of this.'

Chapter 19

It was still fully dark when I woke on Sunday morning. Despite the adrenaline that had been coursing through me the previous evening, mental exhaustion must have won out, because I'd fallen asleep almost instantly, my brain perhaps weary of trying to keep me awake. Something had disturbed me now, however; I just knew I hadn't woken naturally, even though the house was now silent. But there it was again: a very soft rhythmic tapping on our bedroom door.

So, definitely not Daniel. And, in any case, he was likely to sleep for hours yet, coming down from whatever concoction of drugs he'd been on. It all came back at me in a rush then – him turning up in that car, his swagger, his attitude and my impotent anger. The increasingly untenable nature of our situation. And then something else hit me: Molly! It must be Molly who was knocking on our bedroom door.

I slid from the bed, quietly – Mike really needed his lie-in – and tiptoed over to the door. And when I opened it, there she was, in her pyjamas, her little hand raised to knock again.

'Is it alright to be up?' she asked politely. 'I'm really thirsty.'

'Of course, sweetie,' I whispered. 'Let me just get my dressing gown.'

As I followed her down the stairs, I was struck once again by just how pale and wraithlike Molly was. If there was one thing I could do for her in the short time we were going to have her, it was to feed her on demand.

Having taken Molly downstairs and supplied her with a big tumbler of milk, I settled her down on the sofa and put the television on for her while I made her some breakfast – boiled eggs and soldiers, and plenty of it. And she'd probably want a second meal when we had ours, I mused. She really did have the proverbial hollow legs and it felt good to get some nutritious food inside her.

The water was just coming to the boil when I heard the front doorbell. The new dress, perhaps, that I'd ordered online in readiness for my eldest grandson Levi's 17th birthday in November, for which we'd planned a big family meal out. And, brought by a lark of a delivery driver, I realised, as I went off to answer it because it wasn't yet half past six. Were they even allowed to start deliveries so early?

But it wasn't a delivery driver, as far as I could tell, since the lad in front of me – a young man in, at most, his early twenties, wearing a tracksuit and battered trainers – seemed to have no vehicle and had nothing in his hands either. He was also shuffling from foot to foot, as if agitated about something.

'Is Deejay there?' he asked me.

'It's six thirty in the morning,' I answered, noticing how dishevelled he was. Tall, but very skinny, as if he'd not eaten properly in days. 'He's in bed,' I said. 'Who are you?'

'Well, you'd best get him up,' he said, the agitation in his body now accompanied by an unpleasant angry grimace. 'He owes me two hundred fuckin' bar and I want it.'

I felt strangely unintimidated by this string bean of a lad. And very irritated too. 'Listen,' I said, squaring up to him, 'I don't care what he owes you. It's nothing to do with me and I'd like you to leave before I call the police.'

'I'm going nowhere, lady,' he snarled back. 'Trust me, yeah? Not till I get my fuckin' money.' He then plunged a hand into one of the tracksuit bottoms' big baggy pockets and when he withdrew it, there was something in his hand. I couldn't see it at first but then there was an audible click, and something that *did* intimidate me caught the light by the front door. A knife. He'd actually pulled a knife on me.

The shuffling of his feet intensified as I stared at it. It was only small, but it was pointed, and a knife was still a knife. 'You get me?' he asked, and there was something in his eyes that now really scared me. They were narrowed, unfocussed, like he was high on something. Or coming down from something. Either way, I got the sense that even he didn't know what he might do next. 'Like I say, lady,' he finished, 'I am going fuckin' nowhere.'

'Oh, I think you'll find you are, son.'

Mike's voice, from behind me. I hadn't heard him approach and felt a rush of relief. Closely followed by a new fear, that my husband hadn't seen the weapon.

'He's got a knife, Mike,' I said, shrinking back a little. 'And—'

'He's got a *pen*knife,' he said dismissively, moving forwards to properly fill the doorway with his bulk. 'You back off right now, lad, or I'll move you myself. Like the lady said, it's nothing to do with us. How did you get this address, anyway?'

Perhaps stunned by Mike's apparent lack of concern about the blade, the lad took an immediate couple of steps backwards. Perhaps, in his world, a show of disdain like that meant his adversary almost certainly had a bigger weapon, and no qualms about using it, either. Plus, I realised one of Mike's hands was out of sight, behind the door. In any event, the lad suddenly looked a lot less cocky. He flicked the blade closed and shoved it back in his pocket, his gaze darting left and right and the foot dance increasing, as if he was now questioning his wisdom in even coming here. He then jabbed a finger in our general direction.

'How do you fink?' he spat, from his now-safer distance. 'You fink we're stupid or summat? You best tell him Si called, and he best get my dough sorted, or *he's* getting sorted. You tell him. And it's not just me who's after him, neither. Tell him that!'

He walked backwards down the path, with a rock frontman's swagger, then spun around at the gate and headed off down the street, one middle finger held aloft until he was almost out of sight.

All the air left my lungs in one enormous relieved outbreath. 'What the *hell*?' I began, as Mike closed and chained the door. 'Christ, he could have *stabbed* you!'

'Or *you*,' said Mike, and I could see from his expression that he'd been every bit as scared as I had.

'And that wasn't a penknife!' I couldn't help but point out. 'Good God, did that really just happen? Oh my God,' I went on, still trying to take it in, 'bloody drug dealers know where we live, Mike!'

At which point we both turned to go back into the kitchen, to find Molly standing there, tumbler in hand. 'Was that,' she asked, 'one of the medicine mans?'

'No, darling,' I said, guiding her towards the table, 'it was a silly boy who had lost his way. Me and Mike, we just told him where he had to go.'

Mike raised his eyebrows and gave me a wry grin. 'We certainly did, and that's teamwork, Molly. And now,' he added, 'I think Casey might put those cartoons on a bit louder for you and close the door while she makes your chucky eggs.' He looked at me then, his intentions clear. 'While I go upstairs and give Dan an unexpected wake-up call, too.'

Knowing what was probably to come, I shut the door as instructed. Then, in a moment of inspiration, went to fetch the headphones I used with my tablet when I was travelling by train or air. 'Pop these on, love,' I said, 'so I can listen to the radio,' which, happily, she accepted without comment. I then, still with a sense of complete unreality, went back to preparing her eggs.

Once they were done, I told Molly that, as a special treat, she could eat them in front of the telly, it being further away from the noise of whatever hullabaloo was about to start upstairs. And was glad I did, because it started up almost immediately. And, with Molly now occupied, eyes and ears only for the telly, I told her I was nipping to the loo, then shot straight upstairs, anxious that things could escalate and that I might need to be there.

With Daniel's door open, I could see straight away that it already had. He and Mike were standing in the middle of the room, squared up to one another, practically nose to nose.

'What you gonna do, big man?' Daniel yelled. 'My boys would knock you the fuck out, man!'

'Get out of my face,' Mike said, seemingly rooted to his spot. 'Your boys, from what I've seen, couldn't knock the skin off a rice pudding, kiddo. Now, I've said what I've said and that's that. No more idiots at our door, *ever*, do you hear me? Because I'm telling you right now, Dan, you're all out of chances here, mate.'

Daniel sucked air in through clenched teeth and

looked Mike up and down in a highly provocative way. For a moment I thought things might now get physical, but Daniel clearly thought better of it because he took a step back. 'Pussyoh!' he snapped. 'Pack my gear, innit? Simples. I don't need this shit.'

'No, Dan, and neither do we,' I said, deciding this was probably the time to step between them. 'Nobody here is impressed with your mouth,' I told him. 'So, you want out? Okay then. You leave that with me, lad. Let's see what can be sorted.'

I slipped my hand into Mike's and he squeezed it as he took it, then we both left the room and headed back down the stairs.

'God, Case,' he whispered, 'I am *sick* of this.'

Thankfully, Molly was still in cartoon world and since she was still working her way through her eggs and soldiers, we retreated to the kitchen area and made a much-needed coffee. So much had happened and the sun was only just up!

'No doubt he'll fall straight back to sleep,' Mike said. 'And without another thought about what's just happened. He's probably still high, in fact, being woken up at this time.'

'It's all that stupid street talk that got me,' I said. 'That's new, for sure. He's definitely picked up with some new friends, and none of them any good. Bloody cars turning up here, stupid lads, presumably dealers, demanding money, pulling knives. What the hell are we doing?'

Mike got the milk out of the fridge and placed it down on the counter. 'Not putting up with this crap any longer. *That's* what we're doing. First thing tomorrow, Casey, you phone Christine, tell her we've had it and want him gone. We've struggled on for long enough, and, you know, we don't get any better thought of. It's just like "Oh, the Watsons will do it, they always do it!" Well not this time. And I'm not having anyone pull a bloody knife on my wife!'

'Poetry in motion,' I quipped, trying to lighten the mood a little. 'But I thought you said it was only a penknife?'

Mike shook his head and frowned. I think we were both more shaken than we realised, but at the same time, I couldn't help but feel a big whoosh of relief. We'd reached our red line finally. The decision had been made for us. No more procrastinating. No more dithering. No more seeing how things went. We were all at risk now, not just Daniel.

The boy himself slept for the rest of the day and that suited everyone. While Mike spent most of it in the garden – it was bright, even if cold, and he wanted to be outside – I spent much of it playing with Molly, who was like a bottle of pop after Riley came over with the promised bag of toys. She didn't stay, though, as she had to drop her youngest, our 10-year-old granddaughter Marley Mae, to a friend's house, and, perhaps for the only time ever, I was glad of it. I really didn't want to tell my daughter about what had happened, it would only worry her. And, if she'd stayed, I might have been unable to stop myself.

'Is it Christmas?' Molly asked, once Riley had gone and we began delving into the toy bag. I thought she might be joking, but I could tell she was in earnest. And I realised that it was now only a matter of weeks away.

'No, not quite yet,' I said. 'But it very soon will be.' And in that moment I could so easily project myself forward. *To* Christmas. And, given how things were beginning to look, that there was a fair chance Molly would still be here.

'But we could pretend it is, couldn't we?' she asked, looking at me hopefully and grabbing both my hands.

'Of course we can,' I told her, feeling the prickle of impending tears. I was like a bottle of pop myself, I realised, though for very different reasons.

Since we were having a roast chicken dinner anyway, I decided to go the whole hog, fashioning some pigs in blankets and checking the use-by date on my cranberry sauce, and a form of Christmas dinner was duly served at the end of the day. By this time, we knew Daniel had finally surfaced, due to familiar thumps and bangs coming through the ceiling. But, in a break from the norm, we wouldn't be insisting that he join us. I was fairly sure he wouldn't want to eat with us, in any case, and given the events of the morning, which were still on my mind, that was absolutely fine by me.

But the question was academic anyway. He was still fast asleep by the time the meal was ready, so when I dished up our dinners I made him up a plate. The three of us then enjoyed our early Christmas dinner, Mike and I both aware, though neither of us voiced it, what a pleasure it was to sit down and eat a meal without Daniel's scowling, non-communicative presence. And if Molly missed him, she certainly didn't say so.

The thud of rap music started up around seven. And, with no sign of him appearing for the next 30 minutes, I took the opportunity of Mike needing to nip out and buy some milk for Molly to microwave the dinner and take it up to him. I didn't want to risk them having another confrontation when he returned. But what I'd thought was a smart move was anything but. He looked at me blankly from underneath the duvet as I walked across the bedroom and set it down on his bedside cabinet.

'Chicken dinner,' I said neutrally. 'I imagine you're probably starving. So—'

'I can't do this,' Daniel growled. 'I can*not* fucking do this.' Then, to my utter astonishment, he reached out, picked the plate up and hurled it across the room.

It missed me by inches. 'What the hell is *wrong* with you?' I demanded. 'Are you high?'

'Am I *fuck*!' Daniel yelled. 'I'm coming down and I *need* something! Now!'

I stared at him, angry and confused. 'What are you talking about?' I asked. '*What?* What do you need?'

Daniel jumped up from the bed then and began hopping around. Like the lad on the doorstep, he couldn't seem to keep his feet still. He was clearly highly agitated and was starting to scare me.

'I need money,' he said. 'That's it. You *have* to give me money!' Then he lurched towards me, stabbing a finger towards my chest. 'I need something to take the edge off! You *have* to give me *money*! I need money, or I'll kill myself, I swear I will!'

I stepped back and at the same time tried my best to calm him. But the shuffling and hopping and ranting continued, and I realised he wasn't even seeing me properly; his eyes were unfocussed, his movements erratic. He now started pacing, from wall to wall to wall, each of which he punched, hard, before moving to the next, his bare feet squelching into the remnants of his dinner.

I tried two more times to calm him, saying, 'Shhh, Dan, sit down.' But it was if he had forgotten I was even there. And, by now, I could hear Molly calling up to me, plaintively – the fact that she hadn't come up to find me speaking volumes. She was obviously very scared. So, I backed out from the bedroom, feeling a complete and utter idiot. What had I been thinking, going up to him while Mike wasn't there? I ran back down the stairs, to a trembling, sobbing Molly, and was still in the process of cuddling her tightly on the sofa when Mike returned.

'No, don't go up there,' I said, once I'd given him an edited version of what had happened. 'Let's just leave it, let him sleep it off.'

'Love, we can't just *leave* him. He's coming down from something. Goodness only knows what's going on up there. At the very least, we need to know he's okay.'

Overruled, and probably rightly, I could only sit with Molly while Mike went upstairs to check on the current state of play. But when he returned, moments later, he seemed reasonably happy that all was okay. 'He's sat scrolling on his phone,' he said. 'On the bed, headphones on. Had his back to me, didn't even seem to notice I was there.'

'So, should we, you know, call someone?' I asked, conscious of Molly still beside me and having to choose my words carefully.

Mike shook his head. 'Not yet. Let's just wait for a bit. Whatever state he's got himself into, he's clearly got himself out of. Anyway,' he added, brandishing the milk carton, 'some milk, Molly, love, before bed?'

With Molly distracted by the thought of a glass of warm, frothy milk, we were soon able to coax her back with her cartoons and headphones. Which was where she would stay, at least for the foreseeable. No way was I taking her upstairs to bed.

'But what if he has a seizure or something?' I asked Mike. 'Should we not call a doctor out, just in case?'

Mike considered for a moment. 'It's Sunday evening,' he reminded me. 'If he takes a turn for the worse, we call NHS Direct. Or I take him down to A&E myself, I guess. But he was sitting on his phone, love. Let's just keep an eye, eh? God,' he said with feeling, 'I am sick of all this. But I tell you one thing, I don't think we're done with this day yet.'

And just like the saying, no truer word was spoken. Just 10 minutes later, we heard the now-familiar sound of Daniel's feet thumping on the stairs. Mike raced into the hallway, but the front door was already open, Daniel running down the path to a waiting car. It was the same BMW he'd emerged from before and he was headed towards it, whooping and laughing hysterically. Having barely stopped, the car immediately zoomed off again.

So, once again, it was time to get on my mobile. Make the same phone calls, to the same people, only to be told the same things. That Daniel wasn't technically missing, but that they'd put it on their system, that information would be uploaded, that I would be kept informed.

In short, as Mike quipped, another Groundhog Day. Tomorrow, though … Tomorrow would be different.

Chapter 20

I woke up on the Monday morning knowing that I'd had a good night's sleep for once. I felt rested and content, and then I immediately felt terrible. Terrible because my principal reaction to Dan not having returned home was one of profound relief. How bad was it that I felt that way? It's not that I didn't still feel anxious about what he must have been up to – I did, because the road he was going down almost always ends badly – but I was, finally, admitting defeat. I had not been able to stop that from happening.

Mike had already left for work – I had not heard him leave – and, having not heard a peep from Molly either, unsurprisingly, I decided I'd start the day with a shower. I did all my best self-talk in the shower and today was no different. *You did everything you could, and more, Casey*, I told myself. *Do not feel guilty about what you're doing here*. I even mused that I could quite possibly have been doing the best thing for Daniel. If there were no available carers to take him on in this town, they would have no choice but to reach out to other council areas and maybe he'd end up miles away from all of his current influences by default. Which would give him a fighting chance of a fresh start. It sounded nice, but I doubted that somebody like Daniel would be happy with the prospect of a new life. Not when he was so deeply embroiled in this current one.

Having been up so late, Molly was still fast asleep when 9 a.m. came around, so I took the opportunity to phone Christine and tell her what Mike and I had decided. I filled her in on the weekend's events, and hearing her sighs and groans, I felt pretty sure she knew what was coming. 'So, I'm afraid that's it for us, Chris,' I finished. 'I'm so sorry. But he'll have to go, and ideally as soon as possible.'

'I absolutely cannot blame you,' Christine said. 'You have done all you could – gone above and beyond, to be honest – and we cannot ask for more. I'll get on to Phoebe now and come back to you.'

My relief that things were now happening turned out to be short-lived, however. Christine called back, as promised, around half an hour later, but not with the news I'd expected.

'I have to tell you,' she began, 'I'm really shocked about this, but I've been told to pass on that you will have to give 28 days' notice to end the placement.'

I was so stunned that for a few moments, I was rendered speechless. 'What?!' I said finally. 'I can't believe you're saying that. Did you tell them what's been going on? About the drug dealer coming round? The knife? Who has told you to say this?'

"The managers, my manager and Phoebe's too, and of *course I* told them,' Christine began. 'I told them everything you've told me. But they're adamant that the 28 days is non-negotiable – fully supported in any way you need it to be, of course, but—'

'But that's ridiculous! What needs to happen? For me to be threatened by a bigger knife? A firebomb to come sailing through our front window?'

'I told you, Casey. I'm shocked myself, but—'

'But what about Molly? What am I supposed to do with her? The poor child's already a complete nervous wreck when he's around, and the way things are heading …'

'Yes, I *know*,' Christine answered, 'but Dan is your main placement.'

This really riled me. 'So what? I was asked to take Molly, I was *pressured* to take her. I told EDT the sort of environment she'd likely be coming into, and that it was far from ideal, and now I've just been left to get on with it – conveniently out of sight, out of mind. It's not on! Where does *her* welfare figure in all this?'

'I *know*,' Christine said. 'It's a terrible situation—'

'An *untenable* situation,' I interrupted. 'I can't stress that enough. And what about Mike? How long is it going to be before the lad physically attacks him? We are *that* close, believe me – he's off his head half the time, so there's no telling what he's capable of. This is *not* on,' I snapped at her. 'I need him gone *now*. I need you to *support* me in this, Christine!'

I could hear my friend gasp. Then a moment of silence. 'I have *always* supported you,' she said quietly, and her tone brought me up short. I had hurt her.

'I'm sorry, I'm sorry,' I rushed to tell her. 'I know that, I'm sorry. I'm under stress. I'm just stunned that they'd think it was okay to leave us in this situation.'

'I don't think they think that. I *know* they don't think that. But, look, right now he's AWOL anyway, so at least there's that ... Look, how about I go back to them and tell them that if and when he's found, you *will* have him back, but that you'll need him gone within a week? Would that work? Could you just hold on for one more week?'

I really didn't want to, but I also knew I had to concede *something* – offer something for Christine to go back to her superiors with.

'Okay,' I said. 'One week. Assuming he returns. Plus, what about Molly?' I added. 'I was expecting a call this morning about what's going to happen with her, but I've heard nothing yet. To be honest, this morning I was going to tell you that we're happy to help out further with Molly, because we love having her, but wow! No *way* could I subject her to a whole month more of Daniel! But perhaps if it's just the week, then ...'

'There has actually been a development with that,' Christine said. 'Although Molly's mother was found in a known crack house, she wasn't found to be in possession so she was only charged with neglect. The upshot is, she won't be going to prison, at least not yet anyway. She's been given the opportunity to go on a mandatory drug rehabilitation programme. A live-in programme for six weeks. She is also kicking up a fuss about seeing Molly. To be honest, though, it's not got the ring of truth. We think she believes if she acts like this, a judge might be more lenient with her. Anyway, it's not likely, but it is possible that the courts may decide she can have contact with her daughter once the programme is complete, provided there are no issues of drug use while in there. So yes, we'd be grateful if you could hold on to the girl for those six weeks, but we can cross that bridge if and when we come to it.'

'Okay, I'll speak with Mike and get back to you about the six-week thing,' I said. 'He will say yes, I'm sure of it, but the way things have been, I don't want to make any decisions without him being involved. Is that okay?'

'That's more than okay, Casey. And, really, *thank* you. And listen, I completely understand where you were coming from, so don't feel bad about venting at me – that's what I'm here for. And I'll do my very best to bypass that 28 days.'

Though floored by them playing the 28 days' notice card on me in the first place – how could they even suggest it? – with Daniel currently missing, I ended the call feeling reasonably optimistic that we could manage another seven days, even if he was returned to us imminently. Which might yet happen, so it obviously meant my first job of the day would be to deal with something we hadn't had the energy to face the previous night: clearing up the mess in his bedroom.

Which is exactly what I was in the middle of (by now assisted by my pyjama'd little helper, who was very pleased the 'scary man' had gone) – when a flurry of phone calls started coming through. Since I knew it would be a while before Christine called back, I automatically assumed it must be the police and I couldn't help but feel my heart immediately sink, but then, immediately after that, I felt really guilty.

But it wasn't the police, at least not directly. It was Tom Griffin, the drugs counsellor, calling back with some dates. I had to tell him that, sadly, Daniel was once again AWOL and even if he did return, we were throwing in the towel, which, though he wasn't surprised – 'been here many times before, trust me' – obviously made me feel worse.

Second was a call from Mr Hench at the school, hoping to thrill me with the news that they could offer Daniel those two extra sessions he'd promised. Once again, I had to let him know that Daniel was missing (similar response – 'c'est la vie'), which reminded me that I'd forgotten to mention to Christine that, it now being Monday and the taxi being due, *that* needed cancelling too.

Which meant I next had to find the number of the taxi firm and tell them not to come. Only minutes after

I'd done that, I got a text from Mikey's mum, Carol, which read: *Still not seen either of the little sods, I'll let you know if they turn up here.* Which of course cemented the fact that my hunch was right and that Daniel was who knew where, with Mikey.

Then Mike, it now being lunchtime, called re the text I'd sent earlier. 'Of course we'll keep her,' he reassured me, but was predictably furious that they'd tried to insist we also keep Daniel for a whole further month. 'What *planet* are they on?' he fumed. 'We've had drug dealers threatening us!' And he insisted that I let him know as soon as Christine called back: 'Because if *she* hasn't come through, then I'm heading right down there. We're at risk, Case. I am *not* having this. Has his social worker rung?'

'Nope,' I said. 'She will know everyone else has, I suppose, and if she's nothing to add, she probably won't want to be on the receiving end of a rant from me about the bloody 28 days thing!'

And then, finally, mid-afternoon, Chris called. She wasn't yet able to confirm that we'd only have to keep Daniel for a further week, but, since he was still missing and might yet not come back, the situation was still hypothetical anyway. 'But I have news about Molly,' she added. 'Have you had a chance to talk to Mike yet?'

'Yes,' I said. 'And he's fine with it. More than happy to keep her.'

'That's brilliant,' she said. 'And she's had a social worker allocated. And a proper care plan for the next six weeks is being put together as I speak. Plus, if you're happy to do so, feel free to go ahead and approach your local school. It seems her school attendance up to now has been, at best, patchy, so the sooner we can get that in place, obviously the better.'

'Will do,' I said, thinking how nice it would be to take care of Molly over the coming weeks. And how much nicer it would be, I couldn't help feeling at the same time, without Daniel in the mix. I felt terrible thinking that, of course, but I couldn't lie to myself. 'And, please, Chris,' I asked, 'do your best with the 28-day thing. Because if he *does* come back, this is not going to be the place for her.'

Chapter 21

Christine came good: we were only required to keep Daniel for another week. But the situation remained hypothetical. As I'd expected, his bedroom sat empty that night. And the next night. And the next night as well. And a text exchange with Carol proved both fruitless and depressing: Mikey was home. No, she didn't know where Daniel was, but if found, and he turned up on her doorstep *ever* again, she'd be calling the police.

It felt as if we were living in a strange kind of limbo; we had no idea where Daniel was, what he was doing, whether he was even still in the area, but every time my phone rang, I was braced for the news that they'd found him and were bringing him back to us.

'But they agreed a week,' Mike reminded me, before leaving for work on the Thursday morning, 'so even if they call you today to say they've found him, we've only got to hang in there for four more days.'

Breaking Point

And fingers crossed they wouldn't, I couldn't help but keep thinking. We'd committed to Molly now and she was settling in well. And there was next to no chance that, if Daniel *was* returned to us, he'd skip up to his room, plop his headphones on his head and spend the rest of his stay playing shoot-'em-ups with his gaming friends. Quite the opposite. The longer he was away doing whatever he was doing, the more likely it was that he'd be returned in an even worse state.

So, when my phone did ring, late afternoon, while I was washing up Molly's tea things, I almost feared looking at the screen. It was an unknown number. Which meant what? Any number of possibilities. So, since Molly was playing happily on the floor with the battered Barbies, I slid open the patio door into the darkening garden. We'd had such a nice day, and I was keen that that continued, so I didn't want her hearing anything that might unsettle her.

'Oh hello, is that Casey?' the female caller asked. 'My name's Chloe Warden. I'm the new allocated social worker for Molly. I'm just calling to introduce myself and check how things are going.'

'Ah, hello,' I said, the anxiety draining a little. She sounded young, very cheerful. Not yet drained by her caseload. 'And, yes, things are going well – well, as well as can be expected, given our circumstances at the moment.'

'Yes,' Chloe said, 'I've heard all about the other child you have in. Quite the challenge, I understand.'

'And then some,' I said. 'But he's not here at present; went on the missing list on Sunday and we haven't seen or heard from him since. A bit of a worry, of course, but it's at least meant that Molly has had the chance to see us in our natural environment rather than us having to constantly fend off confrontation.'

'Well, my next bit of news may help on that front as well. As soon as I was allocated this morning, I set myself the task of ringing around your local primary schools and the first one I rang agreed to take her. How about that? And it seems it's walkable from where you live as well.'

'I'm impressed!' I said, thinking that this social worker might be exactly what Molly needed. An advocate who meant business and wasted no time in getting things done. 'That was on my list of things do today, and, yes, I know the school – I've had foster children placed there before. When can she start?'

'More good news,' Chloe said, 'because they have space for her right now, so they said as soon as you can sort a uniform out, she can start. I suggested next Monday, will that give you time?'

'More than enough time,' I said, my spirits really beginning to lift now. 'In fact, I already have some bits of their uniform that will fit her, so I only really need to think about getting shoes fitted and letting her choose a new backpack, and I can do that by the end of the weekend. So, is that it, then? I just take her in on Monday morning?'

Breaking Point

Chloe confirmed that I was to take Molly to meet a Mr Gray, a new acting headteacher apparently, at 8.30 a.m. on Monday morning and she also arranged to come out and visit at home so she could explain her role to Molly and get to meet us. She arranged to do this on the Tuesday afternoon after Molly had had the chance to have a couple of days at school.

'I'll leave it till around 4 p.m.,' she said, 'so she'll definitely be back from school, but, of course, if there are any problems with Dan that might affect that, just ring me and we can re-arrange.'

Everything was suddenly looking up and I felt re-energised for the first time in weeks. I couldn't wait to tell Molly all about her new school and as I expected, she was over the moon about it. In fact, she never shut up about it! Bouncing around on the sofa, jumping up to Mike to ask for a spin around and dancing all over the house. She was like a whirlwind and, happy as I was to see that, I could fast feel that new-found energy of mine running out, because I'd been running on empty for so long now. So, I was happy when Mike appeared in the kitchen holding his and Molly's coats, plus gloves and hats, and suggested that I needed a bit of respite.

He turned to Molly. 'I think someone could do with a walk to the park,' he said, 'someone who needs to tire themselves out before bed. Now then, who could that be? I know – Molly!'

'In the dark?' Molly asked, looking shocked at his suggestion. 'My mummy always says I mustn't go out once it got dark. I must stay in and not answer the door.'

We exchanged a look. 'No, it's fine, sweetie,' I reassured her. 'Because you'll have Mike with you, won't you? Come on, let's help you get that coat on, shall we?'

Excited now, Molly couldn't wait to leave the house and I mouthed a heartfelt thank-you to my thoughtful husband.

But I should have perhaps known that the unfinished business that had dogged us all week was still far from over. They were just through the front gate and had turned onto the pavement when a slow-moving car came to a stop outside the house. There were no sirens or lights, but I knew it was a police car just the same; I'd seen enough to just know it. And there in the back, I saw, with a sinking feeling in my gut, was the even more familiar outline of a teenager in a hoodie. Mike had clocked it too and had stopped by the gate, Molly's hand in his. For one awful moment, I thought he was going to turn around and bring her back inside. I shook my head.

'No, Mike,' I called to him, with a shooing motion. I really, really didn't want Molly to be around to witness whatever was about to transpire. 'I'll text you,' I added. 'Wait for my text, okay? And I'm *fine*,' I assured him. 'The police are here, aren't they? Go on. Wait for my text, okay?'

He was reluctant, I could tell, but as Molly didn't seem to have noticed anything, he set off down the road with her towards the park. I waited by the door, pulling my cardigan tightly around my body. I had a chill and I don't think it was from the weather. There was just one officer this time and he opened the back door of the car to let Daniel out.

'Come on, lad, let's have you,' he said, and then, 'Move it, I don't have all day.'

Daniel got out then and glanced at me before lowering his head again. He raised it again as they approached the doorstep. He was filthy and his clothes were ripped. The new clothes that I'd bought him too. I also noticed a fresh black eye, and as he noticed me looking at him, his expression became defiant, bordering on mocking. I stepped aside to allow them both to pass me into the house.

'He's been giving us the right runaround,' the officer said, 'but we found him this morning, shoplifting from a big supermarket. He wouldn't say where he's been staying but we have our suspicions.'

Daniel laughed. 'You know nuffink, blood, d'ya get me? You pigs couldn't stop a robbery in progress if you was shoppin' in there.'

'And you, young man, are straight on the road to jail,' the officer retorted. 'See how gangster you are mixing with the big boys, eh, lad?'

Daniel laughed again and pushed past me to go upstairs, barging against me in the process.

'Get a bath!' I shouted after him, struggling to control my anger. 'You're in a right state.'

'I'm sorry about that,' I said to the officer. 'Has he been giving you hassle all the way back?'

The officer shook his head. 'I think all that was for your benefit,' he said. 'Quiet as a mouse in the car, but he's definitely on something, love. Are you alone in the house?'

I nodded. 'That was my husband with the little girl as you pulled up. They've only gone to the park for half an hour and then he'll be back. Why? Do you think he's likely to kick off?'

The officer shrugged. 'Who knows?' he said. 'Like I said, he's taken something, though not a chance in hell he'll tell us what. He was definitely going wild in the supermarket where we arrested him. Take my advice and just leave him up there.' He nodded towards upstairs. 'Till your husband's home. Don't take any chances, love. No doubt by tomorrow he'll have slept it off and be a different kid. Someone'll be in touch with you about the next steps in the morning.'

As the officer drove away, I stood on the doorstep for a while, thinking of what he'd said. I'd definitely not risk going upstairs after the last time I tried it, not while Mike was out anyway, but I also remembered that last time Daniel hadn't actually been high at all – it was out of his system and he was craving more drugs. Yes, the officer was right: tomorrow he might be a different kid, but not in a good way, I imagined, not at all.

When I came back inside after seeing the policeman off, I could hear the shower running, so at least he was getting clean, but five minutes later I heard the bedroom door slam, and then nothing. I was happy to leave him there sleeping and hopefully it would be for the night.

By the time Mike got back, I'd been upstairs to fetch Molly's pyjamas and already prepared her supper. I scooped her up and took her to the living room.

'I think we'll leave your bath till morning this time,' I said, tickling her sides. 'We're going to get these jim jams on, give you a tray for supper and let you play with your dolls for half an hour before bed, so me and Mike can go fold the ironing pile.'

Molly was thrilled at the prospect of uninterrupted play, but Mike could tell I was stressed.

'What's he done?' he asked. 'And are you okay?'

I told him what the police officer had said and assured him I was okay.

'It's just every time I see him now,' I said, 'I'm expecting chaos – and not just me. Even the officer said to leave him alone because he was clearly on something.'

It was at exactly that moment when the rap music started up, and at a volume that could not be ignored.

'Jesus!' Mike barked. 'Is he for *real*? Leave him alone? How? With that racket going on? And why should we?' he asked me. 'Why is it that he can come home, upset everyone in the house, sleep all day, then torment us all night? We're just enabling his behaviour, Casey, if we allow that. I'm not having it – it's about time that kid was given a reality check.'

'Seriously? Right now? Mike, this is nearly over in any case, so—'

'So, let's just say my one last duty is to maintain the boundaries we're employed to put in place for the kids we care for. And I'm *not* having that racket thumping away overhead.'

He then stormed off upstairs, with me close at his heels.

'No, you wait there, Casey,' Mike said as he turned halfway up the stairs. 'You need to listen out for Molly, I'll be fine.'

I was obviously worried for Mike, but I could see the sense in protecting Molly from any confrontation, so I remained on the stairs, close enough to hear what was going on, on both floors.

'Wakey, wakey!' I heard Mike say, so Daniel was obviously in bed. 'Let's have you up and that music off. It's teatime.'

Daniel grunted something, then shouted, 'Fuck off!'

'Not happening,' Mike said firmly. The music abruptly ceased. 'You got clothes on under there?' he then added cheerfully. 'Oh yes, I see you have. Up you get, lad.'

I heard Daniel mutter something else, and then, more clearly, 'I said, fuck off!' He must have leapt out of bed, I realised, because the next thing I heard was three loud punches on what sounded like the bedroom door.

I ran up to see, disregarding Mike's instructions, and the first thing that confronted me was three large, gaping holes in the door. As I was about to run in, I then heard Molly, obviously hearing all of this, screaming hysterically from downstairs.

'Please, Mike, just leave it,' I begged. 'It's not worth it and one of you is going to get hurt.'

'Go on, Mike!' Daniel taunted, 'Do as the lady says, you fucking pussy boy, and leave me the fuck alone!'

Mike glared at Daniel. 'Don't you see what you're doing? How do you think anyone can keep you safe when you behave this way? You could end up anywhere after us, Dan. Don't you even care what happens to you?'

Daniel laughed and threw a mug, which hit Mike in the chest. 'Don't you get it? I don't fuckin' *care*! Who do you think I'm scared of the most, eh? You, or some bad boys I owe three grand to?'

Mike must have then realised the futility of engaging any further with Daniel, because he turned around and guided me out of the room,

'Come on, let's go see to Molly,' he said. 'She must be terrified.'

Mike was physically shaking by the time we were back downstairs and went straight to the kitchen for a glass of water. He then wiped down his top – it was heavily splattered with whatever had been in Daniel's mug. Meanwhile, I tended to Molly, and as I rocked her and wiped away her tears, the anger bubbled up inside me. I was actually playing a part in adding to this child's trauma and it wasn't fair. Once I'd calmed her down, I sat her on my lap and looked her in the eyes.

'I promise you, Molly, that we won't let that boy hurt you and we won't let him frighten you anymore. He's moving to live with another family, so he'll be leaving here very soon, I promise, okay?'

'Do you pinky promise?' she asked, searching my face to check it was truthful, ''Cos he's too scary, I don't like him no more.'

'I pinky promise,' I said as I looped my little finger around hers.

After I'd settled Molly into her bed, and was sure she was asleep, I sat down with Mike to discuss our next moves.

'I've been thinking,' Mike said, 'and you know what, I think this escalation at home is for our benefit. Dan doesn't know he's due to be taken from us imminently, so I think he actively *wants* us to throw him out so that it doesn't look like he has a choice in the matter. I genuinely believe he owes that gang a load of money and they've scared him badly. You only have to look at his face to see he's had another beating.'

'A bit far-fetched, love,' I said. 'If you're saying they've threatened him that he must stay with us, why would they do that?'

'I've put myself in his shoes, and if it were me, I'd be scared that I was in too deep. And it's clear that once these guys have their hooks into the kids, they make it so there's no way out. Dan has probably told a mate that he's hoping for a move, so he can cut loose, and it's got back to whoever, and they've told him he better stay close enough to continue re-paying his debt. Think about it, he's on a good thing here – he's been allowed complete freedom really – so why on earth would he be turning on us like he does? He wants us to end it so he can say he didn't. He's probably hoping like hell that they move him miles away, so they can't get to him.'

It did make sense, and if that were the case, then Daniel must have been in very real danger, so the end of the seven days – just three left now – couldn't come fast enough.

Chapter 22

Anxious about leaving me and Molly at home without him, the next morning Mike phoned his work and asked for the day off. Luckily, they were very understanding. And I definitely felt a lot happier. It also meant I could take Molly into town, shopping. Since she was due to start school the following Monday, our trip to get the stuff was needed anyway and I was keen to keep her away from Daniel as much as possible.

Before that, though, I needed to call Christine.

And I didn't pull any punches, either.

'I know we said we'd keep him till Monday,' I told her once I was safely out of earshot in the snug. 'But if there's any chance of collecting him before that, can you please, please try to do it? I'm genuinely fearful of further serious violence taking place now and we simply can't cope with it. And it's not just about Molly's well-being and safety. We had another big scene with him when he was brought back yesterday afternoon, properly fronting up to Mike and getting really violent. He was definitely high on something, though who knows what. He then punched three whacking great holes in his bedroom door and Mike's getting to the end of his tether. We can't be dealing with all this, Chris. Not at our age. We need you to send someone to collect him as soon as is humanly possible.'

'I hear you,' she said. 'Leave it with me. There'll be a children's home somewhere who'll take him as an emergency – they'll have to. But that's not for you to worry about. Your safety is the main concern here. I'll get back to you as soon as I can. And listen, keep yourselves safe, okay? Even if it means you all leaving the house and leaving him to it. It's only things, I'd never forgive myself if any of you got hurt.'

'Well, he's asleep at the moment and I imagine he won't wake for hours yet so I'm taking Molly into town for a bit while Mike holds the fort.'

And as soon as I'd said that I was struck by my choice of words. Weren't forts supposed to be places where you kept trouble out? Still, Mike seemed relaxed enough. 'Just go and have fun,' he said, as Molly and I put our coats on. 'I doubt he'll even stir. And in the meantime, I have plans, don't I, kiddo?'

'Plans?' I asked, looking from one to the other. 'What plans might those be?'

Molly, I could see, was grinning from ear to ear. 'That old doll's house,' Mike explained. 'The one I picked up at that boot sale that time. You know, the one I never got around to fixing up for Marley Mae.'

'And I'm going to have it!' Molly trilled, clapping her hands together.

'Oh,' I said. 'Right,' having forgotten it entirely. Then I smiled. 'Well, given the state of it,' I added, now it had come to mind finally – a mouldering old thing covered in cobwebs up in the loft – 'You'll have your work cut out and then some.'

Knowing the nightmare was soon going to be over, I was in a much better place mentally as we drove into town and, excited at the prospect of her very own doll's house, Molly seemed to be too. We'd go to my sister Donna's café, I decided, as we parked. I'd not seen my sister in weeks, and if Molly was going to be staying with us for a bit, they might as well get acquainted.

The shopping didn't take long. Or prove remotely problematic – indeed Molly seemed delighted with everything I suggested. I even had time to buy treats for me and Mike – some perfume for me and some aftershave for him. We were soon settled down in the back of the tearoom, me with coffee and carrot cake, and Molly with a massive ice-cream sundae, made with a great flourish by my sister. It was a taste of how different the coming few weeks would likely be, compared with the last.

I was just dabbing ice cream from the front of Molly's jumper when my mobile vibrated: it was Mike.

I answered it, now fearing some new confrontation.

I was right. 'He's gone,' Mike said, the minute I clicked to answer.

'Gone?'

'Yes, and smashed his whole bloody room up as well!'

Concerned that Molly was listening, I stood up and waved at Donna, who headed over. 'I need to pop outside,' I told Molly. 'To get a signal. But my sister's just here,' I reassured her as Donna slid into my seat. 'And I'll only be a moment …'

Mike was still talking as I went back out onto the lane. 'And when I say smashed,' he said, 'I mean *seriously* smashed. Hang on, let me switch to FaceTime so you can see.'

I watched in horror as Mike appeared on the screen. He looked flushed and he sounded short of breath. He then turned his camera to Daniel's room. He was right, I could hardly believe the amount of damage. The door had been kicked off its hinges, the wardrobe lay on the floor in pieces, obliterated, and the TV had been smashed to smithereens. It looked like blackcurrant squash had been splattered all over the walls and ceiling, and chunks of plaster were even missing from the walls. We'd fostered so many children over so many years and although, yes, a few also attacked their rooms and belongings, I'd never seen anything like this.

'What on earth happened?' I asked as Mike started making his way downstairs, his camera back facing him. 'Dan did all of that on his own? It beggars belief!'

'Who else? I can hardly believe his cheek, but not long after you left, he suddenly appeared in the kitchen, eyes blazing. He said he needed 20 pounds to buy some drugs with – I mean, he actually said those words. I couldn't believe it.'

'I take it you told him no, then,' I said.

'I absolutely told him no. And then the kid went berserk. I mean, like some kind of mad person, screaming and swearing, trying to pull his own hair out. It was surreal to witness. And I tried to remain calm,' he said. 'I swear I did, just kept repeating that he needed to stop, and needed to think about what he was doing. I begged him to stop pulling at his hair, but then he ran off upstairs and by the time I got up there, he was barricading the door. Anyway, it took him only a matter of minutes to do all that damage while I was trying to push the door open, and when I finally managed to get it open – he'd shoved the chest of drawers in front of it – he was like someone possessed. Casey, I mean, *really* bad.

'He screamed at me again for money and I told him there was no chance I'd be giving him cash for drugs, that we should calm down and have a talk about what was happening. But the next minute he was yanking out all the drawers and throwing them at me, then he just shoved me – the strength in that kid, he almost knocked me off my feet! Then he barged past and shot off back down the stairs. And then straight out of the front door. And, of course, I didn't have any bloody shoes on, so by the time I could go after him—'

'You went *after* him?'

''Course I did! Case, he had literally nothing on him. Just a T-shirt and trackies – I can't even say for definite that he had any shoes on! No coat. No money … I mean, where was he going to go? And it's freezing out there!'

I could definitely confirm that, standing out on the street myself, with my own coat inside, hanging over the back of a chair.

'And now my knee is bloody killing me,' he went on, 'and – hang on … What?!'

'What?' I asked.

Mike was by now in the living room. I heard the sound of the patio door being slid back.

'What?!' I said again.

'The shed door, it's hanging open …' he started walking down the garden. 'Maybe he's doubled back …'

'Mike, don't go in there! Just call the police!'

But he was already there. I then heard an expletive my husband almost never uses.

'What?!' I asked a third time. 'What's happened? Is he in there?'

'No,' he said, 'he's not. But the little sod's stolen all my bloody power tools!'

Chapter 23

If things had looked bad in Daniel's room when Mike had been FaceTiming me, seeing them in reality was on a whole other level. It really did look as if a tornado had blown through and the extent of the violence that must have been used to do such damage truly appalled me. Even his beloved PlayStation had fallen victim to his rage. It was still in one piece, but only just.

Having agreed with me that we'd keep Molly out of the way, Mike made her a sandwich and stayed with her downstairs, while I called Christine from the scene of the devastation. But not before I had made a video so she could see it for herself, which, having alerted her to the situation, I texted to her mobile.

'Oh my God,' Christine said, once she'd watched it and called me back. 'This is appalling! What would have possessed him to do such a thing?'

She really needed to ask that? But I refrained from saying so. After all, she was only reacting the way anyone would when faced with such a terrible scene. 'I know,' I said instead. 'I can't believe it, and I'm standing here looking at it. Honestly, in all my years fostering, I have never had a kid do something as bad as this. And that's it, now,' I added, though I probably didn't need to. 'No way is he setting foot in this house again! I honestly don't think I can face any more of this, Christine.' I held my free hand out in front of me. It was trembling uncontrollably. My body confirming that, clearly.

'Oh, good God, no!' she said. 'Absolutely not. And don't worry about calling EDT and the police, we'll do that. Do you have any idea where he might have been headed?'

'Not a clue, but there's something that might have a bearing: he's also broken into the shed and stolen all Mike's power tools.'

'What – run off with them?'

'No, it must have happened earlier. Mike chased him down the street and he had nothing on him, not even a coat. So, we really don't know. But we've been talking about that. He must have done it to try and sell them to get money, mustn't he? Perhaps he stashed them somewhere. Who knows? And we can't say when because we've not been down there in days.'

'Okay, so you'll obviously need to report that to the police,' she said. 'And make an inventory of the loss and damage, because you'll be able to claim for it from us, obviously. And in the meantime, I'll get on to everything else. Anything else missing that you can see?'

'I don't know, I don't think so. I'll check and let you know. I'm beginning to wonder now,' I said, recalling his small hours' cupboard raids. 'As I say, we'll do a very thorough check. And thank you, Christine, I really do appreciate how much you're trying to help us.'

As I went back downstairs and took the coffee Mike had made me, I felt shattered. I *was* shattered. And I could see Mike was too, and while Molly played with her Barbies, seemingly oblivious, thankfully, we both started to question whether we should still be doing a job like this at our ages.

'Are we too old and long in the tooth for this, Mike?' I asked. 'I mean, social services call it experience, but honestly, I'm beginning to think the benefit of that is seriously overrated. Should we really keep doing this? Surely if we can no longer cut it, we're doing the kids that come live with us a disservice?'

Mike shrugged and sighed. 'I don't feel any older than the day we started, love, genuinely.' He pointed to his knee. 'But I know for a fact that we are. When I tried running up that road today, and it all felt so hard, it really got to me. I remember being able to fly down the street after some runaway kid and even be able to lift them up and carry them home, kicking and screaming. No way could I do that these days.'

Despite feeling so shaken, I managed to smile at that thought. 'Well, you definitely couldn't have with a kid of Dan's size, Mike. Not even in your thirties.'

'You know what I mean, Casey,' he said. 'I think our get-up-and-go has finally got up and gone.'

Which was funny, but at the same time, not funny at all. Sad, in fact, to think our 'glory' days might now be far behind us. And it felt sadder still when Molly suddenly appeared in front of us and, without saying a word, climbed up onto Mike's lap and planted a kiss on his forehead.

He grinned at her. 'What's that for?'

She shrugged her tiny shoulders. 'I thought you needed a Molly hug.'

Then she scrambled down again and climbed up to give me one too.

'Awww, thanks, Moll,' I said, 'I think we both needed a Molly hug.'

At which she scrambled down, with a 'you're welcome!' and went back to playing with her toys.

'We *did* sign up for this,' I said to Mike. 'The good and the bad. Old or not, we still know how to do it, and what's needed. It's not our fault if we get a child who won't – or can't – accept our help. Dan was institutionalised and so far down the drugs route, it's going to take a lot more than foster care to help him.'

'You're right, Casey,' Mike said, 'and you know, I think in this case, it's fair to say that it's the system that's ultimately responsible for failing Dan, not us.'

Despite my agreeing to Mike's summing-up of 'the system', I still couldn't help but feel that I'd failed too. I'd made promises I couldn't keep and now Daniel would pay the price. As the weekend passed without hearing anything about the boy, I began to fear the worst. He had no clothes with him, no money, and despite best efforts from the police, who'd searched all his usual haunts, nobody seemed to have a clue where he might be. How could he simply disappear? I couldn't answer that, and nor could I do anything about it – I just had to sit tight and hope I'd soon hear from either Christine or Phoebe.

The one person who wasn't worried, of course, was Molly. No longer fearful that an eruption would take place at home, she was so much happier and practically skipped the whole way to her new school on the Monday morning. I sorted out the paperwork as quickly as I could and then left her to it. There were no tears, no clinging to my leg – in fact, she couldn't wait for me to leave so she could get down to the serious business of making friends. I knew this apparent lack of anxiety was perhaps not as simple as it might seem; she'd been ripped away from everything she knew and this 'bubble' we were currently in was sure to burst someday, but I was happy to take each day as it came and not get ahead of myself. The main thing was that she was settled and apparently happy to be with us, which obviously made me happy too.

I then rushed home to start the business of making Daniel's room look habitable again. Mike had already ordered a new door, which he would pick up after work, and he'd patched up the walls where the chunks of plaster had been gouged out, just as soon as we'd cleared most of the debris. He'd also ordered a skip that was delivered on Saturday afternoon and put all the broken furniture, including the TV, in there, after I'd separated out Daniel's few bits. So, all I had to do was wash the walls and ceiling, re-paint one wall and scrub the carpet. And at least the bed had survived unscathed.

It did hurt me, though, to pack up those things of Daniel's – his beloved PlayStation – now almost certainly unusable – and the two worn controllers, his headset and leads, plus the few items of clothing and footwear he owned. Just the thought that all the material things he had in the world took up no more space than the volume of a mid-sized plastic tub was so depressing. Despite everything, I felt tearful and wished so hard that he'd be found.

It was four days, however, before I heard anything. Then there was a call from Phoebe, just after I'd dropped Molly off at school that morning.

'It's pretty grim, I'm afraid,' she alerted me. 'He's been found in a squat.' She named a district that I'd heard of before. In fact, I was sure I remembered once driving round that area with Mike some years earlier, trying to track down a teenage girl we were looking after. But it didn't matter anyway, I was just keen to hear what had happened.

'An empty house that's obviously been used by addicts for a long time and has now been turned into the base for a gang of county lines dealers, who force kids to work selling drugs all through the night, in return for their fix during the day. I say "fix",' Phoebe elaborated, 'it's much worse than that. They keep them pretty much sedated all the time they're not working and give them very little in the way of food or drink either. Like I say, it's pretty grim.'

'But how did they find him?'

'A tip-off. And it's not just "him" either – it's "them". The police broke in and found four teenagers upstairs, all of them completely out of it; Daniel, plus another lad of around the same age – that Joshua character who'd previously been inside? Plus, two girls, a 14- and a 15-year-old. More edifying, though – if that can be the right word for such an S-H-I-T show – was that they also found two older males, both *compos mentis*, who were arrested at the scene and are now in police custody for a number of county lines offences.'

'What about Mikey?' I asked, fearing the worst for him too. Though I knew he'd returned home after the last time they'd gone AWOL, had he been involved in this too?

'Not him,' Phoebe said. 'At least, as far as I know.'

So there was one shred of good news to hang onto. Perhaps he at least might get back on some sort of track.

'So, what happens now?' I asked, feeling the dread settling in the pit of my stomach. 'With Dan and the other kids? Are they going to get help?'

Breaking Point

'I wish! I mean, down the line perhaps, but for now they've all been charged too, with possession and dealing offences – I know; it breaks your heart, doesn't it? They'll be brought back to court to be dealt with. It's unlikely that any of them will receive custodial sentences, but, of course, they will now have criminal records, won't they?' I heard her sigh.

'Including Dan …' I said. 'Mind you, he's still waiting to be seen in court from the last time, so it's a given for him.' This was a statement, not a question. It had come to pass precisely as we'd feared.

'Yes, but at least he's well away from it all now so that's something.'

'So where is he now? Has he been moved?'

'He has. To another children's home, sadly. But at least it's a reasonably distant one, almost 100 miles away.'

'Thank goodness for that, at least.'

'Well, it's something. Still not quite far enough away, in my opinion, but at least out of the clutches of this particular gang.' She paused and sighed again. There was no trace of her usual brisk tone today. 'He's on a massive comedown, Casey – massive. The full works. I was the one who had to drive him down there, but I had to have an escort to sit with him in the back of the car. It was just horrible – he was sobbing, screaming, kicking the seats, begging us to get him anything we could to take the edge off. He must have been taking all sorts. We're going to try and to get him into some kind of rehab, but it's going to be a fight. I doubt we'll get it, but I'm going to try my very hardest.'

'Well, if anyone can do that,' I told her, 'I'm pretty sure you can.'

'I can only try, can't I? You know me, dogged to the bitter end. He will obviously be allocated a new social worker now he's out of the area, but I've insisted they pass on my number to whoever it may be and allow Dan to phone me if he needs to. It's the least I could do.'

Her choice of words really spoke to me. It *was* a bitter end. And, in all sorts of ways, I felt terrible. Did it have to come to this? Could we have done more? Done things differently? Perhaps I should have also passed on my number, I wondered, would that have been so bad? I wouldn't do it, it was too soon, but maybe in the future.

'By the way,' she added, 'he wanted me to pass on a message. He wanted me to tell you and Mike how sorry he is for what he did at yours. In his words, he was off his head and had no idea what he was doing. He's really sorry for all the damage, *and* for the theft of Mike's tools. Which was not down to him, by the way.'

'What?! You mean he denied it?'

'No, not at all. It just wasn't him who took them. It was one of his cronies – ex-cronies, rather – he just told them where to find them. A last-ditch attempt to square some of his debt.'

'Good lord! Really? But that makes no sense. When?'

'That morning was all a bit of a set-up, as far as I can gather,' Phoebe said. 'Dan chose that moment to go down and confront Mike – it was to keep him busy. He had already arranged for a couple of mates to drive over and pick him up and wait in the car at the end of the street. Apparently, he'd seen the tools in the shed a few weeks back and told these mates about them, so they fixed it up between them. While he was arguing with Mike upstairs, the other lads were in the garden like a flash, forced the lock, grabbed the tools and then waited in the car for Dan round the corner.'

'So, him smashing his room up,' I said, having realised what had happened, 'wasn't *just* about him being off his head, then?'

'Oh, I think he was definitely off his head. But let's just say there was also a bit of method in his madness.'

So, someone else – or more than one someone – now knew where we lived too, great! But it was done, it was over, and at least we were probably no longer of interest. Or, perhaps more likely, given how fast news tends to travel, a place to henceforth keep well away from.

'As you surmised,' Phoebe went on, 'he was just desperately trying to get his hands on something he could turn into ready money – hold them at bay for a bit. Allowing those guys to grab the tools was all he could think of to do that. He knows he can never come back, but he hopes one day you might forgive him.'

'We already have,' I said firmly, because I realised this was true. 'So, if you speak to him again, can you tell him that, from both of us?'

'Of course,' she said. 'I'm likely to be speaking to him next week, I have to go back down there to do the official handover to his new social worker. And for what it's worth,' she added, 'I'm sure he means it, too.'

Chapter 24

I walked up to school to collect Molly that afternoon with my mind full of conflicting emotions. On the one hand, I felt an overwhelming sense of relief that Daniel was safe – it was almost like experiencing a huge mental outbreath, so much so that it made me realise just how wound up with stress I had been. But a big part of me couldn't stop returning to the increasingly nagging conviction that we had failed him, utterly. While, ultimately, the events of the previous couple of weeks had taken matters out of our hands, by that time, hand on heart, there was no getting away from it; I had already checked out emotionally. Already reached a point where I lacked the will to try and help him – something that had rarely, if ever, happened to me before.

It was a difficult feeling to know what to do with. And was perhaps made worse by the comments of everyone around me which, without exception, were supportive, and understanding, and overwhelmingly kind. Of course, we could not have done more than we had. Daniel was addicted to drugs *and* in the clutches of drug dealers, and, given his background, and his refusal to engage, only a physical removal from the whole situation would offer the means to try and change his direction. No, it was clear, to almost everyone but me, it seemed, that this outcome was *always* to be expected.

'You tried your best,' Christine had said to me, via a text, only that morning, once the news had come through to her. 'I'll catch you later,' she promised. 'Here's a virtual hug in the meantime.' So at least she understood what I'd be feeling.

And knew I must continue to feel, at least until the taste of failure wasn't quite so intense. Because, rightly or wrongly, I felt so strongly that they were wrong. I'd moved mountains for kids just like Daniel before – sometimes long after they had been mine and Mike's legal responsibility. I'd done it because I'd been driven to. And driven to because I cared. So, what went wrong this time? How did it work that a deep, deep compassion for this teenager had only fully stirred in me now?

I knew it would help no one for me to wallow this way, but as I walked the few streets to our peaceful local primary, I couldn't help it, and this despite Mike's stern words – *We are not saints, and we cannot have drug dealers knowing where we live, Case!* – still ringing in my ears. Because louder still was the clamour from my conscience: *You never bonded with him. That's the real truth of it, Casey.*

Breaking Point

The primary school looked much like any other primary school at turning-out time. A gated community, these days – how times had changed since my own childhood – albeit one bright with primary coloured play equipment and cheerful, if tatty, bunting, outside which stood pockets of chattering parents, accessorised by buggies and pre-schooler siblings, all wrapped up against the cold. And despite the heavy clouds and the late November chill, the whole panorama felt sunny and optimistic in its vibe. Among those gathered, I knew, there would be troubles and heartaches – parents not coping, financially or emotionally, relationship issues, darker forces at work. It was odds-on, I reckoned, that, among their several hundred pupils, it wasn't just Molly who was a looked-after child. This was just a sad fact of life.

But for the most part – and thank goodness – this was a positive place, where praise was frequently lavished on the children that spent their days here; for doing well at reading, for being kind, being helpful, for passing milestones that, for most, were the normal course of childhood. Where futures, given few had much reason to doubt it, were nothing like Daniel's sorry childhood had been; were expected to be overwhelmingly bright. Happy kids, happy adults, the wider world at a distance. Chips for tea. A bit of tablet time. A bath, book and bed. The world – their small and safe one – mostly rosy.

And in two weeks' time – I'd had the notice, via the school's official WhatsApp – the Christmas Disco would be happening, to which Molly, their newest new girl, was invited. So, I could take heart that, at least for one child in my care, the future was definitely brighter.

The gates unlocked, the crowd dribbled in and formed groups around the playground. And shortly after, the children began coming out. It was not a school I'd ever had a child attend before, but the thought that this was going to become my routine now, for a while at least, couldn't help but lift my mood a little.

It was lifted further when Molly bowled out from her classroom and in the same way she had in the short time since she'd started – full of whoops, smiles and comically wind-milling arms, as if so full of things that she must *absolutely* tell me, her body didn't know where to start.

And so it was, as I braced myself for her to throw herself into my arms, before gathering up all the things she had shed before she did so. Her drink bottle, her book bag, her backpack, her mittens, plus, today, a small drawing she was anxious to show me – of, for whatever reason, a narwhal.

Or 'norwhale' as she described the picture. Which was helpful as it was hard to make out. 'It has a pole on its nose!' she explained breathlessly. 'It's a tusk! But it's not, it's really a giant *tooth*!' she added proudly. 'Oh, and I have a *big* surprise for you, Casey,' she said then, determined to wrestle her lunch box from the backpack I was now holding, before we made our way out of the playground. 'Look!' she said, opening it to reveal what was left. 'My apple core! I ate my *whole* apple – I think I even like apples now!'

I agreed that this was indeed a surprise, and a great one too. 'And, funnily enough,' I said, 'I have a surprise for you too.'

She looked me over, as if assessing whether I carried a concealed treat. 'What is it? Tell me, tell me – what *is* it?'

'You'll have to wait till we're home,' I replied. 'So, we'd better hurry home.'

'Is it a present?'

'It is. And that's all I'm going to tell you. And first, let's pop those mittens back on, shall we?'

Molly duly complied and as we skipped our way home, I felt my spirits begin to inch further out of the doldrums. This little girl coming into our lives had been a gift, I decided. She really was like a balm for my soul. But I wasn't naive. Given what she'd been through, I knew there would be issues to tackle. Doubtless more complex ones too, down the line. But for now, like the child whose hand currently held mine, I would live very mindfully, and determinedly, in the moment and let the process of helping to rebuild her life happen slowly, and steadily, as we did so.

The surprise, which Molly fell upon just as excitedly as I'd anticipated, was another collection of toys Riley had promised me, Marley Mae having had another clear-out. She'd left them on her way to work while I'd been catching up on my fostering reports, daily logs and emails – none thankfully involving any more major incident reports.

As well as a couple more Barbies, and a big bag of clothes and accessories, there was also a life-size baby doll, plus all the paraphernalia that tends to go with baby dolls – a potty, a crib, a collection of outfits, a toy highchair and a little buggy – all, as with the doll herself, deemed 'too babyish' to play with by my now 10-year-old granddaughter.

For Molly, who I now felt absolutely sure had had very little in the way of playthings, this unexpected bounty was treasure. As soon as she was out of her school uniform, and while I started preparing tea, she set herself up in the living room area, fussing over the doll with such tenderness, and also such confidence, that it almost brought a tear to my eye. Was the mothering instinct in some little girls that instinctive? Or had the arrival of the baby doll triggered a memory, even if completely unconscious, of a time in her young life when she too had been mothered, before her own mum's descent into drug use and neglect? Either way, it was heartening to witness. Unlike Daniel, this little girl had come into care while still young enough that the scars she carried could hopefully be healed enough that she had a decent shot at a happy future.

As it turned out though, Molly had a slightly different memory.

'Ah,' I said, as she lay the doll gently in the little crib. 'Are you putting the baby to bed now?'

Molly nodded as she placed the blanket carefully over her. 'Yes,' she said. 'She's tired. She's had a busy, busy day. Shhh, Livvie ...' she cooed. 'It's time to go to sleep now.'

'She's called Livvie, is she?' I asked, as I grated cheese for pasta. 'That's nice.'

'It's not her *proper* name,' Molly corrected me immediately in that bossy way six-year-olds sometimes do. 'Her proper name's Olivia.'

'Well,' I said, playing along, 'that's a nice name as well.'

'Mummy didn't like it,' she said, equally promptly. 'That's why she always called her Livvie.'

I looked up and smiled, assuming this must be part of her make-believe. 'Mummy did? As in your mummy?'

Molly nodded, then smiled, almost to herself. 'What shall we doooo,' she trilled at the doll, 'what shall we doooo, Molly Moooo? What shall we doooo, Livvie Loooo?'

'That's nice,' I said again, imagining a moment of tenderness between mother and daughter being remembered. 'So, what happened to your dolly?' I asked, making a mental note that I should really ask if we could access any of Molly's possessions. I'd not yet heard anything about retrieving any of her stuff and a few bits from home might be comforting for her. I had no clue if this was even possible any more, though, as it had been some time now since they'd been at the house. Surely if it had been a council house, or privately rented, it would have been cleared out and re-allocated by now. I made a mental note that I would have to check it out.

Molly looked at me now, as if confused.

'Livvie loo wasn't a *doll*,' she said, almost indignantly.

This was unexpected. 'Oh,' I said. 'So, Livvie was a real baby?'

Now it was Molly's turn to look surprised. 'Of course,' she said immediately. 'She was my baby sister.'

I took the pasta off the heat, drained it and added the pile of cheese to it, my mind all the while whirring with possible scenarios. *Was my baby sister*. Molly was an only child, wasn't she? Yes, definitely. No dad. No siblings. Just her and her mum. No other family located as yet. And then I noticed that Molly's expression had changed. She was chewing her lip now, looking anxiously up at me.

'Oh,' I said lightly, 'I didn't realise you had a sister.'

'Because you're not supposed to know,' she said, her voice a tiny thing now. 'I'm not supposed to tell. It's a secret.'

'That's okay,' I said, mind going into overdrive. This definitely didn't feel like make-believe any more. 'I'm good at keeping secrets,' I added, keen to reassure her. 'So, there's no need to worry, your secret's safe with me. But where's Livvie now?' I asked. 'Where did she go?'

Molly shrugged. 'I don't know. She *was* there, but one day …' She shrugged again. 'She wasn't …'

'So, she lived with you?'

Breaking Point

Molly nodded and I could see her eyes were shining now, with tears. 'But you mustn't tell,' she whispered. 'Not to anyone. I'll be in trouble.'

'Sweetheart,' I said to her, coming round from the kitchen area to comfort her, 'you are not in any trouble.'

But could this be true? The notes from social services were clear: Molly was her mother's only child. But if there *was* another daughter, where was she?

I felt the stirrings of something I couldn't quite put a name to. But perhaps I didn't need to. All I knew for sure was that I was determined to find out …

Epilogue

A year after Daniel left us, I received an unexpected phone call. It had been a busy year. Mike had had his knee op and recovered, and was even back playing football, and our lives had been particularly full. So, when the name Phoebe popped up on my phone screen, I initially struggled to remember who it was. As soon as I heard the voice, though, I remembered and braced myself, fearing the worst.

'Please tell me Dan is okay,' was the first thing I said. I often thought of him – the guilt had lifted, but I still had that sad sense of unfinished business and, of course, I couldn't help but think the worst.

'Don't worry,' Phoebe said. 'In fact, he's more than okay. That's why I'm calling.'

She went on to explain that after fighting for six months to get rehab for Daniel, and a suitable placement, they had finally secured the funding to get him the help he desperately needed. After three months in a specialist drugs and alcohol rehabilitation unit, he had been placed with five other teenagers in a secure unit just on the border with Scotland.

'He's thriving there, Casey,' Phoebe said. 'Everything is done on site; he's learned how to cook and clean, he's completed his education, and now he's doing a plumbing course. Honestly, he's just loving life. I could cry with happiness every time I see him.'

I was over the moon, and especially when Phoebe told me that Daniel wanted to write to me.

'Of course he can,' I assured her. 'I'd love to hear from him.'

'You can visit him if you'd like to,' she added. 'I go once a month – I could take you if you want to come with me. Don't feel obliged, though. I'm sure he'd be happy just to hear from you.'

So, we've started corresponding and so far, so good. It's early days still, of course. I've learned that things can – and still do – go wrong with kids who've had such a bad start in life, but I'm very hopeful right now and that's pleasure enough.

Oh, and as for Molly and the little sister she'd told us about – well, of course, that's a whole other story …

Breaking Point

A Note on County Lines Gangs

Here, I thought I'd share some helpful facts about county lines, taken from the Met Police website (www.met.police.uk/advice/advice-and-information/cl/county-lines/). If you believe you, or a vulnerable person, child or adult, is at immediate risk from these gangs, call 999 and report it. If you suspect county lines drug dealing is happening in your area, or you know someone is being exploited but don't believe they're in immediate danger, call 101 and report it.

County lines is the name given to drug dealing where organised criminal groups (OCGs) use phone lines to move and supply drugs, usually from cities into smaller towns and rural areas. They exploit vulnerable people, including children and those with mental health or addiction issues, by recruiting them to distribute the drugs. This is often referred to as 'drug running'. Criminals may also use a vulnerable person's home as their base of operations. This is known as 'cuckooing'.

Signs to look out for

There are several signs to look out for that may indicate someone is involved in county lines:

- repeatedly going missing from school or home and being found in other areas

- having money, new clothes or electronic devices but they can't explain how they paid for them
- getting high numbers of texts or phone calls, being secretive about who they're speaking to
- decline in school or work performance
- significant changes in emotional or physical well-being.

Social media

Criminal networks use social media to groom and recruit children for county lines. They may send them direct messages (known as 'DMs'), or share messages to wider groups as 'stories' or 'posts'.

Ways OCGs use social media
- advertising drugs through photos, emojis and price lists
- posting statuses that show money, new drugs or when a dealer is open for business
- dealers sharing 'stories' to followers and using social platforms to expand their network with 'suggested' friends
- tricking people with 'fast cash' scams, which are often referred to as 'squares'. Victims may end up working for no little or no money, which is known as 'debt bondage'
- advertising for 'workers' or 'runners' to recruit people into county lines activities

- using hashtags linked to drugs
- using emojis as code for drug, violence and sexual activities, e.g. the snowflake emoji (buying cocaine), eight-ball emoji (buying an eighth of an ounce) or the rocket emoji (purity of drugs).

Cuckooing

OCGs often use high levels of violence and intimidation to protect the 'county line' and control them. One of these forms of control exploits vulnerable people by using their home as a base for dealing drugs, a process known as 'cuckooing'. Dealers often convince the vulnerable person to let their home be used for drug dealing by giving them free drugs or offering to pay for food or utilities.

Often OCGs target people who are lonely, isolated, or have addiction issues. It's common for OCGs to use a property for a short amount of time, moving address frequently to reduce the chances of being caught.

There are several signs to look out for that may indicate someone is a victim of cuckooing:

- frequent visitors at unsociable hours
- changes in your neighbour's daily routine
- unusual smells coming from a property
- suspicious or unfamiliar vehicles outside an address.

Casey Watson

Missing persons linked to county lines

Children and young people involved in county lines may go missing or be out of touch for long periods of time. During these times, they may be at risk of harm or violence.

If you are reporting a child as missing, you should look out for signs they may be getting exploited. You should note:

- transport they may be using
- people they may be with
- people they may be in contact with.

Parents and carers, stay vigilant!
Love Casey x

CASEY WATSON

One woman determined to make a difference.

Read Casey's poignant memoirs and be inspired.

A FAMILY FRIEND

Sammy has been in care since he was nine years old. Left feeling entirely alone, he has never had a proper safe haven.

There is one person looking out for Sammy: his neighbour 'Uncle Kenny'. But while Sammy may turn to Kenny for comfort, alarm bells soon start to ring for experienced foster carer Casey Watson.

LITTLE GIRL LOST

Kelly suffers with bipolar disorder, and when she attempts to burn down the family home it becomes clear that her six-year-old daughter Amelie is in grave danger.

When she arrives at the home of foster carer Casey Watson, Amelie acts much younger than her age. Casey must get to the root of her behaviour, while doing what she can to keep the family together.

I WANT MY DADDY

Five-year-old Ethan is brought to Casey in the middle of the night after the sudden death of his young mother from a drug overdose

When arrangements are made for Ethan to see his dad in prison, Casey recognises the name and face . . . It turns out she's far more familiar with this case than first imagined.

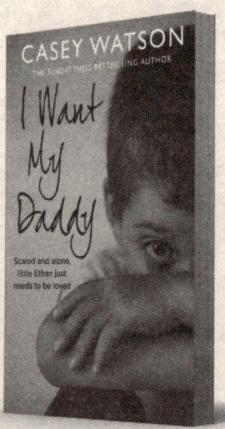

I JUST WANT TO BE LOVED

Casey has fostered her share of vulnerable adolescents, but 14-year-old Elise brings unique challenges

When Elise makes some dark allegations against her mum, Casey doesn't know what to believe. Is Elise telling the truth? Casey is determined to find out and keep her safe.

MUMMY, PLEASE DON'T LEAVE

When baby Tommy – born in prison – and his half-brother, Seth, are placed in the Watsons' care, their troubled teenage mother soon follows suit

Can Casey find the energy and strength to see this unusual case through?

LET ME GO

Harley is an anxious teen who wants to end her own life, and there's only one woman who can find out why

Casey makes a breakthrough which sheds light on the disturbing truth – there is a man in Harley's life, a very dangerous man indeed.

A DARK SECRET

A troubled nine-year-old with a violent streak, Sam's relentless bullying sees even his siblings beg not to be placed with him

When Casey delves into Sam's past she uncovers something far darker than she had imagined.

A BOY WITHOUT HOPE

A history of abuse and neglect has left Miller destined for life's scrap heap

Miller's destructive behaviour will push Casey to her limits, but she is determined to help him overcome his demons and give him hope.

NOWHERE TO GO

Eleven-year-old Tyler has stabbed his stepmother and has nowhere to go

With his birth mother dead and a father who doesn't want him, what can be done to stop his young life spiralling out of control?

GROOMED

Keeley is urgently rehomed with Casey after accusing her foster father of abuse

It's Casey's job to keep Keeley safe, but can she protect this strong-willed teen from the dangers online?

THE SILENT WITNESS

Bella's father is on a ventilator, fighting for his life, while her mother is currently on remand in prison, charged with his attempted murder

Bella is the only witness.

RUNAWAY GIRL

Adrianna arrives on Casey's doorstep with no possessions, no English and no explanation

It will be a few weeks before Casey starts getting the shocking answers to her questions...

MUMMY'S LITTLE SOLDIER

Leo isn't a bad lad, but his frequent absences from school mean he's on the brink of permanent exclusion

Leo is clearly hiding something, and Casey knows that if he is to have any kind of future, it's up to her to find out the truth.

SKIN DEEP

Flip is being raised by her alcoholic mother, and comes to Casey after a fire at their home

Flip has Foetal Alcohol Syndrome (FAS), but it soon turns out that this is just the tip of the iceberg...

A STOLEN CHILDHOOD

Kiara appears tired and distressed, and the school wants Casey to take her under her wing for a while

On the surface, everything points to a child who is upset that her parents have separated. The horrific truth, however, shocks Casey to the core.

THE GIRL WITHOUT A VOICE

What is the secret behind Imogen's silence?

Discover the shocking and devastating past of a child with severe behavioural problems.

A LAST KISS FOR MUMMY

A teenage mother and baby in need of a loving home

At 14 Emma is just a child herself – and one who's never been properly mothered.

BREAKING THE SILENCE

Two boys with an unlikely bond

With Georgie and Jenson, Casey is facing her toughest test yet.

MUMMY'S LITTLE HELPER

A young girl secretly caring for her mother

Abigail has been dealing with pressures no child should face. Casey has the difficult challenge of helping her to learn to let go.

TOO HURT TO STAY

Branded 'vicious and evil', eight-year-old Spencer asks to be taken into care

Casey and her family are disgusted: kids aren't born evil. Despite the challenges Spencer brings, they are determined to help him find a loving home.

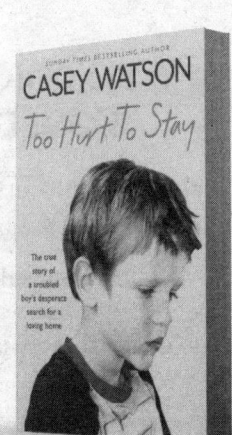

LITTLE PRISONERS

Abused siblings who do not know what it means to be loved

With new-found security and trust, Casey helps Ashton and Olivia to rebuild their lives.

CRYING FOR HELP

A damaged girl haunted by her past

Sophia pushes Casey to the limits, threatening the safety of the whole family. Can Casey make a difference in time?

THE BOY NO ONE LOVED

Five-year-old Justin was desperate and helpless

Six years after being taken into care, Justin has had 20 failed placements. Casey and her family are his last hope.

TITLES AVAILABLE AS E-BOOK ONLY

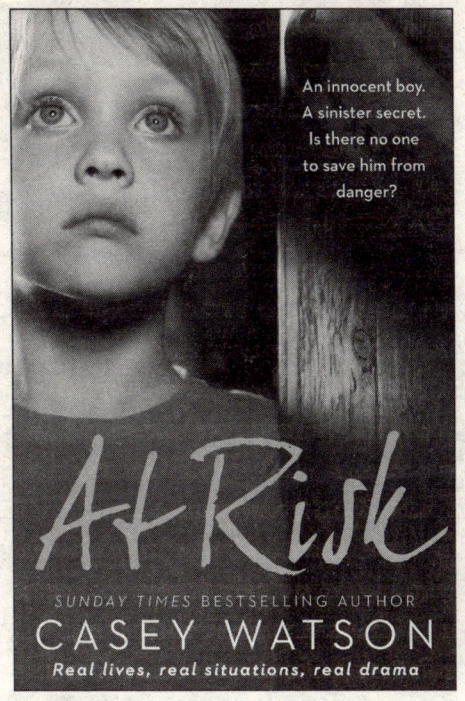

AT RISK

Adam is brought to Casey while his mum recovers in hospital – just for a few days

But a chance discovery reveals that Casey has stumbled upon something altogether more sinister...

THE LITTLE PRINCESS

Six-year-old Darby is naturally distressed at being removed from her parents just before Christmas

And when the shocking and sickening reason is revealed, a Happy New Year seems an impossible dream as well ...

DADDY'S BOY

Paulie, just five, is a boy out of control – or is he just misunderstood?

The plan for Paulie is simple: get him back home with his family. But perhaps 'home' isn't the best place for him ...

THE WILD CHILD

Angry and hurting, eight-year-old Connor is from a broken home

As streetwise as they come, he's determined to cause trouble. But Casey is convinced there is a frightened child beneath the swagger.

NO PLACE FOR NATHAN

Nathan has a sometime alter ego called Jenny, who is the only one who knows the secrets of his disturbed past

But where is Jenny when she is most needed?

SCARLETT'S SECRET

Jade and Scarlett, 17-year-old twins, share a terrible secret

Can Casey help them come to terms with the truth and rediscover their sibling connection?

JUST A BOY

Cameron is a sweet boy who seems happy in his own skin – making him rather different from most of the other children Casey has cared for

But what happens when Cameron disappears? Will Casey's worst fears be realised?

FEEL HEART.
FEEL HOPE.
READ CASEY.

Discover more about Casey Watson.
Visit www.caseywatson.co.uk

Find Casey Watson on f & X

MOVING
Memoirs

Stories of hope, courage and
the power of love...

Sign up to the Moving Memoirs email and you'll
be the first to hear about new books, discounts,
and get sneak previews from your
favourite authors!

Sign up at

www.moving-memoirs.com